OH NO! NOT ANOTHER 1000 JOKES for KiDS

by
Michael Kilgarriff

WARD LOCK LIMITED·LONDON

© Michael Kilgarriff 1983

First published in Great Britain in 1983
by Ward Lock Limited, 82 Gower Street,
London WC1E 6EQ, a Pentos Company.

Reprinted 1983 (four times), 1984 (three times)

All Rights Reserved. No part of this publication
may be reproduced, stored in a retrieval system,
or transmitted, in any form or by any means,
electronic, mechanical, photocopying, recording,
or otherwise, without the prior permission of the
Copyright owners.

House editor Suzanne Kendall
Text set in Times by Avocet Marketing Services

Printed and bound in Finland

British Library Cataloguing in Publication Data

Kilgarriff, Michael
  Oh no! not another 1000 jokes for kids
  1. Wit and humor, Juvenile 2. English wit
  and humor
  I. Title
  828'. 91402'0809292 PZ8.7

ISBN 0-7063-6259-4

Contents

Acknowledgments

After the remarkable successes of *1,000 Jokes for Kids* and *1,000 More Jokes for Kids*, Suzanne Kendall of Ward Lock asked me to compile a third collection. I would like to thank all my friends and acquaintances, and especially my daughter Rebecca and her pals, for allowing me to badger them yet again for funny stories. My grateful thanks are also due to the following:

The Headmaster, Mr V. S. McQueen, the staff and pupils of Montpelier Middle School, London, W5; the Headmistress, Miss M. J. Percy, of Notting Hill and Ealing High School (G.P.D.S.T.), and Miss Ross and the girls of Skipton House; the children of Portsmouth, Cardiff, Glasgow and Dorset; the members of Gemini Theatre Company and their director, Liz York; the girls of 3rd Ealing (Christ the Saviour) Guide Company and their Captain, Mrs Margaret 'Magpie' Lyall; the Headmaster, Mr J. Nisbett and the children of Blagh Primary School, Coleraine, Northern Ireland; Mrs Sylvia Merrikin (Akela) and the boys of 8th Ealing Cub Pack; the Headmistress, Mrs Ashe, and Mr Peter Farrington and the boys and girls of Uxendon Primary School, Kenton, Middlesex; Mr David Lewis (Captain) and the boys of 10th Ealing Coy., The Boys' Brigade; and finally to Mr P. Rankmore (Lieutenant in Charge) and the boys of 4th Ealing Coy., The Boys' Brigade.

Michael Kilgarriff
January 1983

The Bookworm's Banquet

or Literary Lunacies

My Golden Wedding	*by* Annie Versary
The Insurmountable Problem	*by* Major Setback
Crime Does Not Pay	*by* Laura Norder
A Load Of Old Rubbish	*by* Stefan Nonsense
Bilious Attacks	*by* Eva Lott
Tape Recording Made Easy	*by* Cass Ette
Don't Go Without Me	*by* Isa Cummin
Making The Most Of Life	*by* Maxie Mumm
Making The Least Of Life	*by* Minnie Mumm
When Shall We Meet Again?	*by* Miles Apart
The Arctic Ocean	*by* I.C. Waters
Scalp Disorders	*by* Dan Druff
Willie Win	*by* Betty Wont
Return Of The Prodigal	*by* Greta Sonne
A Call For Assistance	*by* Linda Hand
Pain And Sorrow	*by* Ann Guish
Garden Design	*by* Lily Pond
Crossing The Road	*by* Luke About
Sunday Service	*by* Neil Downe
The Laser Weapon	*by* Ray Gunn
Fade Away	*by* Peter Out
Into Battle	*by* Sally Forth
Nappy Making	*by* Terry Towel
Sweet Remembrance	*by* Valentine Card
The Japanese Way Of Death	*by* Harri Kari
Repairing Old Clothes	*by* Fred Bare
Flag Day	*by* Ada Charity
The Lady Artist	*by* Andrew Pictures
The Leaky Tap	*by* Constant Dripping
Summertime	*by* Clement Weather
The Lighthouse	*by* Eddy Stone
Don't Wake The Baby!	*by* Elsie Cries
The Worst Journey In The World	*by* Ellen Back
Knocked For Six	*by* Esau Stars
The Strongman	*by* Everard Muscles
My Happiest Day	*by* Trudy Light
Karate For Beginners	*by* Flora Mugger
Are You A Millionaire?	*by* Jonah Lott
Pig-Breeding	*by* Lena Bacon
Who Killed Cock Robin?	*by* U. Dunnit
Kidnapped	*by* Caesar Quick
The Haunted Room	*by* Hugo First
The Bad Striker	*by* Mr Goal
Making Weatherproof Clothes	*by* Anne O'Rack
Late Again	*by* Misty Buss
Magic For Beginners	*by* Beatrix Ster
English Folk Customs	*by* Morris Dancer
Making Snack Meals	*by* San Widge
Discipline In The Home	*by* Wilma Child Begood
How To Cure Rheumatism	*by* Algy Pan

Cross-Purposes

What do you get if you cross...
—*a skunk and an owl?*
   A bird that smells but doesn't give a hoot!

—*a cow and a camel?*
   Lumpy milkshakes!

—*a sheep-dog and a bunch of daisies?*
   Collie-flowers!

—*a parrot and an alligator?*
   Something that bites your head off and says 'Who's a pretty boy?!'

—*a parrot and an elephant?*
   Something that tells everything it remembers.

—*an elephant and peanut-butter?*
   Either peanut-butter that never forgets or an elephant that sticks to the roof of your mouth.

—*a sheep-dog and a plate of jelly?*
   Collie-wobbles!

—*a football team and ice-cream?*
   Aston Vanilla.

—*a zebra and a donkey?*
   A zeedonk.

—*a kangaroo and a mink?*
   A fur jumper with pockets.

—*a sheep and a rainstorm?*
   A wet blanket.

—*a pig and a zebra?*
   Striped sausages.

—*a centipede and a parrot?*
   A walkie-talkie.

—*a cow and a duck?*
   Queam Quackers.

Differences of Opinion

What's the difference between...

—*the Prince of Wales and a tennis ball?*
One is heir to the throne and the other is thrown into the air.

—*seasickness and an auction?*
One is the effects of a sail and the other is the sale of effects.

—*a cat and a comma?*
A cat has claws at the end of its paws and a comma has a pause at the end of its clause.

—*an orchestral conductor and an oven?*
One makes the beat and the other bakes the meat.

—*a country bumpkin and a welsh rabbit?*
One is easy to cheat and the other is cheesy to eat.

—*a flea-bitten dog and a bored guest?*
One is going to itch and the other is itching to go.

—*a good darts player and a violin-case?*
One finds the middle and the other minds the fiddle.

—*an oak tree and a tight shoe?*
One makes acorns and the other makes corns ache.

—*a young lady and a fresh loaf?*
One is a well-bred maid and the other is a well-made bread.

—*a coyote and a flea?*
One howls on the prairie and the other prowls on the hairy.

—*a hungry man and a greedy man?*
One longs to eat and the other eats too long.

—*a gutter and a bad fielder?*
One catches drops and the other drops catches.

—*a stubborn donkey and a postage stamp?*
One you lick with a stick and the other you stick with a lick.

—*a farmer and a dressmaker?*
One gathers what he sows and the other sews what she gathers.

—*an iceberg and a clothes-brush?*
One crushes boats and the other brushes coats.

—*a kangaroo and a lumberjack?*
One hops and chews and the other chops and hews.

—*a footballer and a well-behaved schoolkid?*
One times passes well and the other passes the time well.

—*sixteen ounces of butter and a loud pianist?*
One weighs a pound and the other pounds away.

—*an elephant and a biscuit?*
You can't dunk an elephant in your tea.

—*an old car and a classroom?*
Not a lot — they both have a lot of nuts and a crank in the front!

—*a robber and a church bell?*
One steals from the people and the other peals from the steeple.

—*a girl and a postage stamp?*
One is a female and the other is a mail fee.

—*a satirist and a clock-maker?*
One takes the mick and the other makes the tick.

—*a sick cow and an angry crowd?*
One moos badly and the other boos madly.

—*a hill and a pill?*
One goes up and the other goes down.

Elephantasia

Why are elephants bad dancers?
  'Cos they have two left feet.

What do you do if an elephant sneezes?
  Get out of the way!

What happened to Ray when he was stepped on by an elephant?
  He became an X-Ray.

When do elephants paint their toe-nails red?
  When they want to hide in strawberry jam.

What did the grape say when an elephant stepped on it?
  Not much — it just gave a little w(h)ine.

What's the best way to raise an elephant?
  Put her on a fork-lift truck.

How do you get an elephant into a telephone box?
  Open the door.

Is it difficult to bury a dead elephant?
  Yes, it's a huge undertaking.

What would you do if an elephant sat in front of you at the cinema?
  Miss most of the film.

Why do elephants have flat feet?
  From jumping out of tall trees.

Is the squirt from an elephant's trunk very powerful?
  Of course — a jumbo jet can keep five hundred people in the air for hours at a time.

How do you make an elephant sandwich?
  First of all you get a *very* large loaf...

Why don't elephants eat Penguins?
  'Cos they can't get the wrappers off.

What did the elephant say when the crocodile bit off his trunk?
  'I thuppothe you think thad's fuddy...'

What's big and red and hides its face in the corner?
  An embarrassed elephant.

Why did the elephant cross the road?
  To pick up the squashed chicken.

Why do elephants wear sandals?
  To stop their feet sinking in the sand.

Why do ostriches bury their heads in the sand?
  To see all the elephants who aren't wearing their sandals.

How do you get an elephant in a matchbox?
  Take out the matches first.

Why did the elephant take two trunks on holiday?
  One to drink through and the other to swim in.

What do you do with a blue elephant?
  Cheer him up.

If you shoot a white elephant with a white gun, what do you shoot a pink elephant with?
  No, not a pink gun — you paint the elephant white then shoot it with a white gun...

What's grey and wrinkled and lights up?
  An electric elephant.

What do elephants do in the back of a Mini?
  Play squash.

What are the largest ants in the world?
  Eleph-ants.

Sick Humour

or Fits of Laughter

Doctor: 'How is your husband's lumbago?'
Wife: 'Not too good. I rubbed his back with whisky like you told me to and he broke his neck trying to lick it off!'

'Doctor! Doctor! I keep thinking I'm a soft drink!'
  'I told you not to play squash.'

'Doctor! Doctor! Everyone keeps throwing me in the dustbin!'
  'Don't talk rubbish.'

'Doctor! Doctor! I'm boiling!'
  'Just simmer down.'

'Doctor! Doctor! I feel like a snooker ball!'
  'Go to the end of the queue.' (cue)

'Doctor! Doctor! Will this ointment clear up my spots?'
  'I never make rash promises.'

Doctor: 'I'm sorry, Mr Hassleblatt, but I've got bad news. However, I've also got good news. Which would you rather hear first?'
Patient: 'Tell me the bad news first, doctor.'
Doctor: 'The bad news is that we've got to take both your legs off. The good news is that the chap in the next bed wants to buy your slippers.'

Doctor: 'Say one-hundred-and-one.'
Patient: 'Not ninety-nine?'
Doctor: 'Well, everything's going up.'

Doctor: 'And how are you now, Mrs Trample?'
Patient: 'Well, doctor, you know you told me to take half a pint of orange juice every night after a hot bath?'
Doctor: 'Yes?'
Patient: 'I managed to drink the orange juice all right but I've had an awful time trying to get the hot bath down.'

'My doctor told me to take two of these pills on an empty stomach.'
  'Did they do any good?'
  'I don't know. They keep rolling off in the night.'

'Doctor! Doctor! I feel like a needle!'
   'Yes, I see your point.'

'Doctor, I think I've got flu.'
   'Very well. Just put your tongue out and then stick your head out of the window.'
   'Will that make me better?'
   'No, but I can't stand the woman living opposite...'

'Doctor! Doctor! My sister thinks she's a lift.'
   'Tell her to come in.'
   'I can't. She doesn't stop at this floor.'

A man went to the dentist, sat in the chair and immediately began shouting and screaming. 'What's all the fuss about?' demanded the dentist. 'I haven't touched your tooth yet.'
   'I know,' said the patient, 'but you're — aagh! — standing on my foot!'

'Doctor! Doctor! I feel I'm a goat!'
   'Stop acting like a little kid.'

'Doctor! Doctor! I've just swallowed four red snooker balls, three pink snooker balls and two black snooker balls!'
   'Eat some greens and you'll soon be all right.'

'Doctor! Doctor! I've just swallowed a roll of film!'
   'Let's hope nothing develops.'

'Doctor! Doctor! Can you help me out?'
   'Certainly. Which way did you come in?'

'I'm sorry to bother you, doctor, but it's my old Dad. He keeps saying he wants to die.'
   'You did the right thing in sending for me.'

'Tell me straight, doctor, is it serious?'
   'Well, I wouldn't start watching any new serials if I were you.'

'This is a most unusual complaint, Mrs Quilch. Have you had it before?'
   'Yes, doctor.'
   'Well, you've got it again!'

A man rushed into the doctor's surgery, jumped on the doctor's back and began shouting 'One! Two! Three! Four.'
   'Wait a minute!' yelled the doctor, struggling to free himself. 'What do you think you're doing?'
   'Well, doctor,' said the eccentric man, 'they said I could count on you!'

'What seems to be the trouble then, Mr Worryalot?' asked the psychiatrist.

'It's like this doctor,' said the patient. 'I have a huge mansion in the country, two Rolls-Royces, my children go to the most exclusive public schools and my wife is dressed by the finest couturier in Paris.'

'So what's the problem?'

'I only earn £40 a week!'

'I don't think much of that new doctor.'

'Why not?'

'Old Charlie Evans went to see him the other week. He tapped Charlie's knee with that little hammer and his leg fell off!'

'The trouble is,' said the entertainer to the psychiatrist, 'that I can't sing, I can't dance, I can't tell jokes, I can't act, I can't play an instrument or juggle or do magic tricks or do *anything!*'

'Then why don't you give up show-business?'

'I can't — I'm a star!'

'One of my uncles was a doctor, but he gave it up.'

'Why?'

'He just didn't have the patients.'

'Doctor! Doctor! I feel like a racehorse!'

'Take these pills every four furlongs.'

'Doctor! Doctor! I feel like a bee.'

'Buzz off — I'm busy, too!'

'Doctor! Doctor! I've eaten a pencil! What shall I do?'

'Use a pen.'

'Doctor! Doctor! I'm a burglar!'

'Have you taken anything for it?'

'Doctor! Doctor! I keep seeing double.'

'Sit on the couch, please.'

'Which one?'

'Doctor! Doctor! I think I'm a dog.'

'Sit down, please.'

'Oh no — I'm not allowed on the furniture.'

'Doctor! Doctor! I think I'm a telephone.'

'Take these pills and if they don't work give me a ring.'

'Doctor! Doctor! I think I'm shrinking!'

'You'll just have to be a little patient.'

The wife of a man with a wooden leg called at the doctor's and said, 'My husband has broken his wooden leg, doctor. Can you supply him with another?' The doctor duly did so, but a week later she called again. 'My husband has broken his new wooden leg, doctor,' she said. 'Can you supply him with another?' The doctor thought this was rather careless of the one-legged man, but he agreed to supply yet another wooden leg. But when the wife came in the following week for a new leg, and again the week after he grew suspicious. 'That's four new wooden legs your husband has had in the past month,' he said. 'What on earth is he up to?' 'Oh, doctor,' sobbed the wife, 'I can't lie to you any longer. He's making a coffee table!'

'Doctor! Doctor! I feel like a ladder!'
  'Keep calm and let me take it one step at a time.'

A doctor was plagued by one of his patients who happened to live in the house next door. Whenever the patient felt out of sorts he would bang on the wall; at two o'clock in the morning he would shout, 'Doctor! Can you give me something for a headache?' At three o'clock in the morning he would shout, 'Doctor! Can you give me something for a stomach ache?' At four o'clock in the morning he would shout, 'Doctor! Can you give me something for a bad leg?' Eventually the patient died, and the doctor thought that at last he would have some peace, but it was his misfortune to die only a week or two later. And as luck would have it the doctor was buried right next to his complaining patient, and on the night of his burial there came a knock on the side of his coffin and a voice called out, 'Doctor! Can you give me something for worms...!'

A woman went to the doctor complaining of a twig growing out of her head. The doctor examined the growth and gave her some pills. Two weeks later she returned — the twig had grown to a branch with leaves and conkers on it. Again the doctor examined the growth and gave her some pills. But two weeks later she again returned — by now the branch had grown into a sapling and for the third time the doctor gave her some pills. Three months later the woman returned to his surgery. From her head was growing a tree with leaves and conkers, also undergrowth, rocks and a waterfall.
  'Ah, now I know what it is!' said the doctor. 'You've got a beauty spot!'

'Doctor! Doctor! I think I need glasses!'
  'You certainly do, madam. This is a fish and chip shop!'

Grab Bag

One late autumn evening two boys, having collected a sackful of conkers, decided to share them out in a grave-yard. On their way in one of the boys dropped the sack and two of the conkers rolled out. 'We'll get those later,' he said, and in they went to divide up the remainder. As they were counting them out a small girl happened to be crossing the graveyard, and to her horror she heard from behind a bush a voice say, 'One for you, one for me. One for you, one for me!' In terror she rushed to the gate and bumped into a policeman. 'What's the matter, little girl?' he asked, for she was obviously in great distress.

'Oh, Mr Policeman!' she wailed, 'there's ghosts in the graveyard, and they're sharing out the dead bodies! Listen!' And as she held a trembling finger to her lips they heard a voice say, 'One for you, one for me. And we mustn't forget those two by the gate!'

The Teddy Bear had gone to work on a building site clearing the ground for a new block of offices. But he had only been there an hour when he sought out the foreman.

'Someone's stolen my pick!' he said angrily.

'I'm not surprised,' said the foreman. 'Didn't you know? Today's the day the Teddy Bears have their picks nicked!'

'My girlfriend's one of twins.'

'How can you tell them apart?'

'Her brother's got a beard.'

'How do you do?'

'Do what?'

'Throw the baby down!' shouted the man to a woman on top of a blazing building.

'I daren't!' she yelled back. 'You might drop him!'

'No, I won't!' he shouted back. 'I'm a professional goal-keeper!'

Reassured, the woman dropped her baby to the footballer, who immediately bounced it three times and kicked it over the garden wall...

Paddy and Mick went duck-hunting with their dogs but without any success. 'I know what it is, Mick,' said Paddy. 'I know what we're doing wrong.'

'What's that, then, Paddy?'

'We're not throwing the dogs high enough.'

17

A woodcutter, a butcher and a lollipop lady were walking in the woods one day when they got lost. Anxious to find shelter for the night before it got dark they were delighted to come across a little hut in a clearing. 'Let's try there!' said the woodcutter. 'Yes, let's!' said the butcher. But the lollipop lady didn't much like the look of the place — it seemed more than a little sinister and creepy. So when they all arrived at the door she said, 'I'll go round to the side and you two go in first.'

In went the woodcutter, to be pounced on by a witch! 'What is your occupation?' she asked, and when told she immediately took out a huge chopper and cut his legs off! In went the butcher, and he was also captured by the witch. 'And what is *your* occupation?' she demanded, and on being told she took a cleaver and cut his legs off as well!

Then in went the lollipop lady who had seen all these gory doings from a window. 'I'm a lollipop lady,' she declared. 'You'll have to suck my legs off!'

Three biscuits were crossing the road when the first one was knocked down and then a second was knocked down. What did the third biscuit say as he reached the pavement in safety? 'Crumbs!'

'What happens if my parachute doesn't open?' asked the trainee.

'You pull String A,' said the instructor.

'But supposing that doesn't work?'

'You pull String B.'

'But supposing *that* doesn't work either?'

'In that case,' said the instructor with a smirk, 'a great big hand comes down out of the sky, grabs you and puts you down safe and sound. All right?'

The day dawned for the trainee to make his first parachute jump, and sure enough his canopy failed to open. He pulled String A as instructed — nothing! He pulled String B — nothing! But then a great big hand came out of the sky, grabbed him and put him down safe and sound. And as he walked away a great big foot came down out of the sky and squashed him flat...

The inmates of a prisoner-of-war camp asked whether they might be permitted to play a series of football matches against their captors. 'Certainly!' said the Camp Commandant. 'And everyone must practise hard! My men will practise on the bottom field, my officers will practise on the top field, and you prisoners will practise on the minefield!'

'Care to come to my birthday party on Saturday, Jill?'

'Thanks, Trevor. Where do you live?'

'Number thirty-eight, London Road. Just push the bell with your elbow.'

'Why with my elbow?'

'You're not coming empty-handed, are you?'

Postman: 'Is this letter for you, sir? The name is all smudged.'
Man: 'No, my name is Allsop.'

18

'Dark in this cave, isn't it?'
   'Dunno — I can't see to tell.'

Did you hear about the farmer's boy who hated the country? He went to the big city and got a job as a shoe-shine boy, and so the farmer made hay while the son shone!

A stranger walked into a pub and ordered a large brandy for himself and drinks for everyone in the bar. 'And have one yourself,' he said grandly to the landlord. Half an hour later the order was repeated: a large brandy for himself and drinks for everyone in the bar — and one for the landlord. He carried on like this all evening, every half hour ordering drinks all round — and one for the landlord, who eventually became concerned about the size of the bill. So when the stranger attempted his ninth gigantic order the landlord said, 'I hope you won't mind my mentioning it, sir, but your bill now amounts to £168.75p.'
   'Does it?' said the stranger. 'Well, I'm sorry about that, because I haven't got a penny on me!'
   The landlord leapt over the counter in a fury and grabbed the stranger by the throat; he slapped him round the face, kicked him on the shins and finally hurled him out through the door where he landed in a heap in the gutter.
   The following evening the bar had only been open a few minutes when who should come in but the stranger! 'A large brandy for me,' he said, 'and drinks for everyone in the bar. But I'm not giving you one,' he said to the astounded landlord. 'After a couple of pints you turn very nasty...!'

'Imagine you're on a hike,' said the Scoutmaster to Eric the Tenderfoot, 'and you're facing north. Now, what is on your right?'
   'East, Skip,' said Eric.
   'Correct. And what is on your left?'
   'West, Skip.'
   'Correct again. And what is at your back?'
   'Er — my rucksack, Skip.'

Sign in shop window:
FOR SALE
Pedigree Bulldog.
House trained. Eats anything.
Very fond of children.

Advertisement in newspaper:
WANTED
Lad to trace gas leaks with
lighted candle.
Must be willing to travel.

'How old were you last birthday?'
   'Nine.'
   'I see. So you'll be ten on your next birthday.'
   'No, I won't. I'll be eleven.'
   'How can that be?'
   'I'm ten today.'

'That girl looks like Helen Green.'
'She looks even worse in red.'

'There's a man outside with a big bushy beard.'
'Is it a naval beard?'
'No, it grows on his chin.'

Two boys were watching television when the fabulous face and figure of Bo Derek appeared on the screen. 'If ever I stop hating girls,' said one to the other, 'I think I'll stop hating her first.'

'What shall I sing next?'
'Do you know "Loch Lomond"?'
'Yes, I do.'
'Then go and jump in it!'

'I've got over 5,000 records.'
'Over 5,000! Gosh, you must be very fond of music.'
'Oh, I don't play them. I just collect the holes in the middle.'

'What steps would you take,' roared the sergeant-instructor, 'if one of the enemy came at you with a bayonet?'
And a small voice in the rear rank muttered, 'Dirty great *big* ones!'

'Why were you late back to camp, Frank?' asked the Scoutmaster.
'I'm sorry, Skip,' replied the Scout. 'But as we crossed that field of cows my beret blew off and I had to try on forty before I found it.'

An old soldier was visiting the site of one of his past battles. 'I remember this spot so vividly,' he said to his wife, his eyes misting over with nostalgia. 'It was just here that my Commanding Officer fell.'
'Was he shot?' she asked gently.
'No. Blind drunk as usual.'

Flying instructor: 'Tomorrow you will fly solo.'
Trainee pilot: 'How low?'

'Yesterday my sister threw pepper in my face.'
'Golly! What did you do?'
'Sneezed.'

How do you stop a cold going to your chest?
Tie a knot in your neck.

'This morning,' said one pilot to the other, 'I made a perfect three-point landing.'

'That's nothing,' came the reply. 'This morning I made a perfect one-point landing.'

'How did you manage that?'

'I got stuck on the church steeple!'

'My neighbours bang on the wall at all hours.'

'Doesn't that keep you awake?'

'No, but it doesn't half interfere with my trumpet practice!'

'Is that Cohen, Cohen, Cohen & Cohen?'

'Yes, madam.'

'May I speak to Mr Cohen, please? It's very important.'

'I'm afraid Mr Cohen is on holiday.'

'Oh...may I speak to Mr Cohen, then? It's extremely urgent.'

'I'm afraid Mr Cohen is off sick.'

'Oh, dear...what about Mr Cohen? It's a matter of life and death!'

'Mr Cohen is in Brussels on business.'

'Oh, Lord, I'm desperate!' Can I speak to Mr Cohen, then?'

'Speaking.'

'Why are you jumping up and down?'

'I've just taken my medicine and I forgot to shake the bottle.'

'This morning my Dad gave me soap-flakes instead of corn-flakes for breakfast!'

'I bet you were mad.'

'Mad? I was foaming at the mouth!'

'Did you hear about Charlie Evans' diet? The doctor said he could only have bananas and coconut milk. For three months that was all he had — bananas and coconut milk!'

'Did he lose any weight?'

'No, but he can't half climb trees!'

'Some girls think I'm handsome,' said the young Romeo, 'and some girls think I'm ugly. What do you think, Sheila?'

'A bit of both. Pretty ugly.'

'Why are you covered in bruises?'

'I started to walk through a revolving door and then I changed my mind.'

Top of the pops:

She Left Her Electric Blanket On, And Now She's The Toast Of The Town

Don't Throw The Cat In The Washing-Machine, Mother, Or You May Get A Sock In The Puss

They're Moving Father's Grave To Build A Sewer

Meet Me Under The Clothes-Line, Darling, 'Cos That's Where I Hang Out

Vesuvius Please Don't Blow Your Top, or, Lava Come Back To Me

'You have to be a good singer in our house, you know.'
  'Why's that?'
  'There's no lock on the lavvy door.'

Did you hear about the woman who dreamed she was chewing her pillow?
  In the morning she was all right, just a little down in the mouth.

'Is it possible to eat soup politely with a big moustache?'
  'Yes, but it's a big strain.'

'I'd like to buy a dog.'
  'Certainly, sir. Any particular breed. A red setter, perhaps?'
  'No, not a red setter.'
  'A Golden Labrador?'
  'No, not a Golden Labrador. I don't want a coloured dog. Just a black and white one.'
  'Why a black and white one, sir?'
  'Isn't the licence cheaper?'

As the fire engine pulled away from the station with its siren blaring — DA! *Da!* DA! *Da!* DA! *Da!* — the crew became aware of a boy running alongside. The fire appliance accelerated, surging through the traffic — DA! *Da!* DA! *Da!* DA! *Da!*—but still the lad managed somehow to keep up. Eventually the driver turned on to a motorway where he could put his foot right down, but still the boy was there running alongside!
  Mile after mile the fire engine tore along — DA! *Da!* DA! *Da!* DA! *Da!* — but the boy miraculously kept pace with the speeding vehicle. His superhuman running finally unnerved the driver, who, despite the urgency of the call, slowed and stopped. 'Hey, sonny!' he shouted to the boy who had also stopped. 'What in blazes do you want?'
  'A 30p Mr Whippy, please,' came the reply, 'and no chocolate flake!'

A lady in a pub noticed a man in the corner of the bar rapidly getting drunker and drunker. 'I've seen you in here before,' she snapped at him, 'and you're always drunk. Why do you drink so much?'
  ''Cos o' my problem, lady,' he said mournfully as he downed another double Scotch.
  'And what problem do you have, may I ask?'
  'I drink too much.'

'You're ugly!'
  'And you're drunk!'
  'Yes, but in the morning I'll be sober!'

Good news! I've been given a goldfish for my birthday... the bad news is that I don't get the bowl till my next birthday!

Good news! At school today there will be free Coca-Cola for everyone...the bad news is that the straws are 50p each!

Good news! My Dad's just bought me a smashing model railway engine...the bad news is that he forgot to buy the track!

A man unable to stop himself stealing asked the doctor for help and advice.
'Try these pills,' said the doctor. 'They should help.'
'But what if they don't?' asked the wretched patient.
'Then see if you can get me a video, will you?'

1st Eskimo boy: 'Where's your Mum come from?'
2nd Eskimo boy: 'Alaska.'
1st Eskimo boy: 'Don't bother — I'll ask 'er myself.'

The new Guide was asked by her father whether she learned how to tie any knots.
'Oh, yes, Dad,' replied the keen Guide. 'And next week we're going to learn how to untie the Captain!'

'Last winter during the dark nights I dressed all in white so that the traffic would see me.'
'Did that keep you safe?'
'No. I got knocked down by a snow-plough.'

'Young man,' said the old lady to the Boy Scout, 'can you see me across the road?'
'I dunno,' replied the lad. 'I'll go and have a look.'

'When's your birthday?'
'August 26th.'
'What year?'
'Every year.'

Why is a tree surgeon like an actor?
'Cos he's always taking boughs.

Which burns longer — a black candle or a white candle?
Neither. They both burn shorter.

'That new restaurant has an interesting item on the menu.'
'Oh — what's that?'
'Soup in a basket!'

Advertisement in the window of a dry-cleaners:
We'll clean for you   We'll press for you
We'll even dye for you

Advertisement in the window of a chemist's:
Got a cold? Try Chesto Cough Drops
We guarantee you'll never get better

Why did the golfer wear an extra pair of trousers?
 In case he got a hole in one.

Supporter: 'I know you lost ten goals to nil but why did you have to clout that little boy?'
Footballer: 'He's our good luck mascot!'

'Want to try some of this? I've just invented it.'
 'What is it?'
 'My new truth drink. One sip and you tell the truth.'
 'All right, I'll have a go...ugh! That's paraffin!'
 'And that's the truth!'

'Do you like this dress? It's seventy years old!'
 'Did you make it yourself?'

A boy riding his bicycle knocked over an old lady; she wasn't hurt, just shaken up and furious. 'You wretched boy!' she fumed, dusting herself down. 'Don't you know how to ride that bike?'
 'Yes,' he replied, 'but I don't know how to ring the bell!'

What did the fireman's wife get for Christmas?
 A ladder in her stocking.

Which Member of Parliament has the biggest head?
 The one with the biggest hat!

Why did the cowboy die with his boots on?
 'Cos he didn't want to stub his toes when he kicked the bucket.

What did the judge say to his wife when he came home?
 'It's been another trying day.'

'*What does a boy do when he wears his trousers out?*
 Wears them in again.

How many famous people were born in Dundee?
 None — only babies.

'Even when my pocket's empty I've still got something in it.'
 'What's that?'
 'A hole!'

24

'Do you like my new swimming-pool?'
   'It's marvellous. Must have cost you a fortune!'
   'Yes, it did at that.'
   'But why isn't there any water in it?'
   'I can't swim.'

A man in a cinema left his seat to buy an ice-cream. On his return he said to an old lady sitting at the end of the row, 'Did I step on your toe just now?' 'You certainly did!' she said crossly. 'Oh, good,' came the heartless reply, 'this is my row.'

The woman in a theatre box-office was surprised one evening just before the show at the behaviour of a patron. He bought a ticket, went away, and then returned a few minutes later to buy another one; he went away again, returned and bought a third ticket. Then he went away yet again, returned yet again and bought a fourth ticket. By this time the show had started, so the woman in the box-office said, 'I hope you don't mind my asking, sir, but why do you keep coming back and buying more tickets?'
   'Every time I try and get into the auditorium,' the hapless patron replied, 'some chap takes my ticket and tears it in half!'

Telephone Operator: 'Is that the lunatic asylum?'
Superintendent: 'Yes, but we're not on the phone.'

'I'm holding a match and a lighter. Which is the heavier?'
   'The match of course.'
   'No, 'cos they're both lighters!'

Two Irishmen looking for work saw a sign which read TREE FELLERS WANTED. 'Oh, now, look at that,' said Paddy. 'What a pity dere's only de two of us!'

A man went into the Post Office with some jelly stuck in one ear and some cream cake stuck into the other. The man behind the counter said, 'Why have you got jelly in one ear and cream cake in the other ear?' To which the customer replied, 'You'll have to speak up — I'm a trifle deaf!'

What do vegetarian cannibals eat?
   Swedes...

The convicted murderer was about to be shot. 'Do you have any last request?' asked the prison warden. 'Yes,' replied the criminal, 'I'd like to sing a song.' 'Very well,' said the warden, and the condemned man began to sing: 'Nine hundred and ninety-eight thousand, three hundred and twenty-eight bottles, hanging on the wall...'

25

'This watch,' said the very superior person, 'is shockproof, waterproof, antimagnetic, and will function perfectly for one hundred years. I paid no less than £400 for it!'

'Did you really?' said his humble friend. 'I bought a watch ten years ago for no more than 50p; two days after buying it I dropped it in the river and its been running non-stop ever since.'

'The watch?'

'No, the river!'

'Are your teeth checked?'

'No, sort of off-white...'

'Why are you so angry?'

'It's all the rage.'

Sign in stationery shop window:
Calendars and Diaries
All with 1 Year's Guarantee

Mr Grouch was enraged when young Joe from next door began throwing stones at his greenhouse. 'I'll teach you, you young imp of Satan!' roared the furious neighbour. 'I'll teach you to throw stones at my greenhouse!'

'I wish you would,' said the cheeky lad. 'I've had three goes and I haven't hit it yet!'

One very hot day an extremely small man went into a cafe, put his newspaper on a table and went to the counter. But on returning with his cup of tea he saw that his place had been taken by a huge, bearded ferocious-looking man of some twenty-two stone in weight and six feet nine inches in height. 'Excuse me,' said the little man to the big man, 'but you're sitting in my seat.'

'Oh, yeah?' snarled the big man. 'Prove it!'

'Certainly. You're sitting on my ice-cream.'

Why is the Isle of Wight a fraud?

Because it has Needles you can't thread, Cowes you can't milk, Freshwater you can't drink, and Newport you can't bottle!

'Why do you keep doing the back-stroke?'

'I've just had lunch and don't want to swim on a full stomach!'

Jemima's new shoes were too squeaky for the irritable librarian, and as Jemima tip-toed past the 'Silence' sign the librarian yelled out, *'QUIIIIEEEEEETTTT!'*

'I'm collecting for the old folks' home. Have you anything to contribute?'

'Hang on and I'll fetch Grandad.'

I wouldn't say Robert is stingy but every time he takes a coin out of his pocket the Queen blinks . . . and he's so suspicious! He doesn't even trust himself — both his eyes watch each other all the time.

'I don't think these photographs you've taken do me justice.'
    'You don't want justice — you want mercy!'

Claud isn't exactly stupid, but when he went to a mind-reader he got his money back.

'I understand you buried your cat last week?'
    'Had to. She was dead.'

The private detective was reporting to his boss. 'I traced the woman to Manchester, sir,' he said, 'but then she gave me the slip. Then I traced her to Glasgow, and again she gave me the slip. I picked up her trail in Cardiff, where again she gave me the slip.'
    'This is getting monotonous, Holmes,' said the boss. 'What happened then?'
    'I found her in Birmingham, sir and there — '
    'She gave you the slip?'
    'No, sir. In Birmingham she gave me the frock.'

Did you hear about the pop-singer who got his shoelaces tangled up in his hair? When he stood up he broke his neck.

'There's a leaky roof in my office.'
    'Won't the landlord repair it?'
    'Repair it? He's so mean he's charging me an extra £5 a week for the use of the shower!'

Did you hear the tragic event at the supermarket? A customer was leaning over the frozen food counter when five fish fingers reached up and strangled him.

'What's that awful ugly thing on your shoulder?'
    'I don't know — what is it?'
    'Your head.'

Why did the stupid man fall out of the window?
    He was trying to iron his curtains.

Why did the stupid man fall out of the tree?
    He was trying to sweep up the leaves.

Did you hear about the woman who was so mean she kept a fork in the sugar-bowl . . . ?

After many years of searching, the wicked Abanazar finally found the magic cave which he hoped would contain the wonderful lamp, the possession of which would make him master of the universe. He stood before the rock which sealed the entrance to the cave, spread his arms wide, and in a commanding voice said 'Open Sesame!' And from within the cave a ghostly voice answered, 'Open says-a who?'

Two boys camping out in a back-garden wanted to know the time, so they began singing at the tops of the voices. Eventually a neighbour threw open his window and shouted down at them, 'Hey! Less noise! Don't you know what the time is? It's three o'clock!'

'Tell me,' said the hiker to the local yokel, 'will this pathway take me to the main road?'
   'No, zur,' replied the rustic, 'you'll have to go by yourself!'

'I didn't come here to be insulted!'
   'No? Where do you usually go?'

'No, no, no!' said the enraged businessman to the persistent salesman. 'I cannot see you today!'
   'That's fine,' said the salesman. 'I'm selling spectacles!'

A very grand lady made her very first visit to a post office—previously one of her servants had always gone for her, but on this occasion curiosity got the better of her, and in she went to purchase a postage stamp. Gazing at the small gummed piece of paper she said haughtily to the clerk,
   'Have I got to stick this on myself?'
   'No, lady', came the reply. 'You stick it on the envelope!'

Two lorries, one carrying a load of red paint and the other a load of purple paint, crashed on a desert island. The drivers are now marooned.

A man just released from prison was so elated after five years behind bars that he ran down the street shouting, 'I'm free! I'm free!' And a small boy on the corner said, 'So what — I'se four!'

Mr Timpson noticed his neighbour, Mr Simpson, searching very hard for something in his front garden. 'Have you lost something, Mr Simpson?' asked Mr Timpson. 'Yes,' replied Mr Simpson. 'I've mislaid my spectacles.' 'Oh dear,' said Mr Timpson, 'Where did you last see them?' 'In my sitting-room,' said Mr Simpson. 'In your sitting-room?' queried Mr Timpson. 'So why are you looking for them in your garden?' 'Oh,' replied Mr Simpson, 'there's more light out here!'

Customer: This restaurant must have very clean kitchens.
Manager: Thank you, sir. What makes you say that?
Customer: Everything tastes of soap!

'Do you know the quickest way to the station?'
Yes — run!'

Think of the numbers two, four, seven, and eight . . . now,
shut your eyes . . . dark, isn't it?!

Behind the counter of a sweet shop served a woman who
was seven feet tall and sixty inches wide. What did she
weigh? Sweets.

A man standing on a canal bridge saw a barge passing below.
What's the bargemaster's name? Watt.

Charlie and Farley saw two men at a river bridge fishing in a
most peculiar manner. One was holding the other over the
parapet by his ankles and the second was hooking the fish
out of the water with his hands! Strange though this angling
technique may have been it was remarkably successful, and
the man being held over the bridge was throwing up big fish
every few seconds. 'Let's try that!' said Charlie to Farley,
and Farley agreed. So on they walked till they came to another
bridge, where Charlie held on to Farley's ankles and waited
for his friend to throw up lots of fish. But five minutes went
by and Farley had caught nothing; ten minutes, twenty
minutes — an hour, then two hours, and still no fish. Then
suddenly Farley called out, 'Charlie, pull me up quick!
There's a train coming!'

But Charlie let go of Farley, who was run over by the train
and seriously injured. 'Charlie!' yelled out Farley, 'don't
just stand there. Call me an ambulance!' 'All right,' said
Charlie. 'You're an ambulance!'

'What are you doing with that manure?' said the nutter to
the gardener. 'I'm putting it on my rhubarb,' replied the
gardener. 'Really?' said the nutter. 'Where I live we put
custard on it!'

In 1800 an Irishman invented the lavatory pan . . . in 1900
an Englishman invented a hole in it . . .

Two men went to the Jobcentre looking for work. The first
was told he would be given a simple test of his abilities.
'Who is the present Queen?' he was asked. 'Er — Queen
Elizabeth the First,' he replied. 'Sorry that's wrong,' said
the clerk. 'It's Elizabeth the Second.'
Outside the man said to his friend, 'They'll ask you the
Queen's name,' he said. 'I'll write it down for you and pin it
inside your jacket.' So in went the second man and again the
clerk said, 'Who is the present Queen?' The second man
looked inside his coat and answered, 'Marks and Spencer!'

A man arrived home after dining at a restaurant to find that
his home had been visited by burglars who had completely
stripped the house — not a stick of furniture was left, no
carpets, not so much as a light bulb remained! Furious at
the loss, the man decided it was his absence at the restaurant
that was to blame. Accordingly he returned to the
restaurant, stuck a gun under the manager's nose and
demanded the contents of the till. 'Oh, surely, sir,' said the
manager calmly, 'your meal wasn't that bad?'

Three men visited a wizard's castle to ask for help. 'If you can spend one hour in my horrible dungeon,' the wizard replied, 'you will be granted your heart's desire. But you have one wish each, and only one, so choose carefully.' In went the first man to the horrible dungeon, to find his nostrils assailed by the most awful, vile smell he had ever experienced. Doing his best to ignore the fetid stench he concentrated on his wish — 'I want to be a doctor! I want to be a doctor!' And sure enough after an hour he emerged a doctor. The second man entered and also managed to think safely of his heart's desire despite the dreadful smell. 'I want to be a lawyer! I want to be a lawyer!' And he too emerged after an hour a fully-qualified lawyer. But when the third man entered he immediately said, 'Pooh!' and straightaway was turned into a bear . . .

News Flash: 1,000 Wigs stolen in Cumbria. Police are combing the area.

Why did the lady have her hair in a bun?
   'Cos she had her nose in a cheeseburger!'

How do you define agony?
   A man with one arm hanging from a cliff-top and an itchy behind!

News Flash: Eminent plastic surgeon dies. He sat on a radiator and made a complete pool of himself.

The salesgirl in a chemist's shop one freezing cold winter's day was surprised to see a small girl come in with bare feet. 'Aren't you chilled with nothing on your feet?' she asked. The little girl looked down and said, 'Oh, I thought I was in Boots!'

Did you hear about the idiot stunt-man who tried to jump over two dozen motor-bikes in a double-decker bus? He might have succeeded but someone rang the bell.

Two children were admiring the famous statue by Rodin entitled 'The Thinker'. 'What do you suppose he's thinking about?' said one, to which the other replied, 'I should imagine he's thinking about where he put his clothes!'

Stan had bravely climbed a tall tree but now found himself unable to get down. 'Why don't you come down the same way you went up? called out his pal.
   'No fear!' shouted back Stan. 'I came up head first!'

'How's your new guitar?'
   'Oh, I threw it away.'
   'Why?'
   'It had a hole in the middle!'

Newsflash: Forty pedigree dogs stolen from kennels. Police say they have no leads.

Tarzan had climbed to the top of a mountain in the middle of the Amazon jungle. At the summit he was immediately surrounded by hideous monsters, ghouls and demons of every kind. Do you know what he said? 'Boy, am I in the wrong joke!'

The workmen had just finished laying a huge wall-to-wall carpet when one of them noticed a small lump right in the centre. 'Oh, those must be my cigarettes,' he declared. 'I was wondering where they had got to.' So rather than take up the carpet and go through the difficult and tedious process of relaying it he simply took a large mallet and banged the offending protuberance flat. Just then in came the lady of the house, carrying a tray. 'I've brought you some tea,' she said. 'And I think one of you left these cigarettes in the kitchen . . . oh by the way, have any of you seen my little boy's hamster?'

Two friends were out hunting grouse. A bird suddenly flew out of the bracken right before their eyes; one of the men raised his gun and fired. The grouse uttered a despairing squawk, its wings folded and it fluttered to the ground. 'You needn't have shot it!' said the other man. 'The fall would have killed it!'

In the swimming competition the first high diver announced that he would attempt a triple somersault with one and a half twists. The second diver arrived on the top board carrying a fish. 'And what are you going to do?' asked the judge, to which the diver answered 'A somersault with pike!'

I Say! I Say!

What did the bull say after his famous visit to the china shop?
  'I've just had a smashing time!'

What did the boy candle say to the girl candle?
  'Let's go out together!'

What did one eye say to the other eye?
  'Between you and me, something smells!'

What did the girl magnet say to the boy magnet?
  'I find you very attractive.'

What did the big clock hand say to the little clock hand?
  'I'll be back in an hour.'

What did the egg say to the Kenwood mixer?
  'I know when I'm beaten.'

What did the calculator say to the bank clerk?
  'You can count on me.'

What did the chick say when she came out of the shell?
  'What an egg-sperience!'

What did the Daddy Shoe say to the Baby Shoe?
  'You'll do in a pinch!'

What did the girl bulb say to the boy switch?
  'Boy, do you turn me on!'

What did the Baby Corn say to the Mother Corn?
  'Where's Pop Corn?'

What did one angel say to the other angel?
  'Halo there!'

What did the picture say to the wall?
  'First they frame me and then they hang me!'

What did the mother crow say to the nestling?
  'If you gotta crow, you gotta crow!'

What did the young porcupine say to the cactus?
  'Is that you, Daddy?'

What did one lift say to the other lift?
  'I think I'm going down with something!'

What did one tonsil say to the other tonsil?
  'You'd better get dressed — the doctor's taking us out tonight!'

What did one wall say to the other wall?
  'I'll meet you at the corner.'

What did the dog say to the cat?
  'Woof Woof!' (What else?!)

What did the orange say to the lemon?
  'Hello, lemon . . .'

What did one flea say to the other flea?
  'Shall we walk or take a cat?'

What did the boy octopus say to the girl octopus?
  (Sing) 'I wanna hold your hand, your hand, your hand, your hand . . .!'

What did the bald man say to the comb?
  'I'll never part with you.'

What did one salt-cellar say to the other salt-cellar after a fight?
  'Shake!'

What did the big fountain say to the little fountain?
  'You're too young to drink.'

What did the beaver say to the tree?
  'It's been nice gnawing you.'

What did the King Egg say to the Bad Egg?
  'I'm going to have you eggsecuted.'

What did the Headmaster Egg say to the Pupil Egg?
  'I'm going to eggspel you.'

What did the big tap say to the small tap?
  'You little squirt!'

What did the small tap say to the big tap?
  'You big drip!'

What did one witch say to the other witch when inviting her to supper?
  'You'll just have to take pot luck!'

What did one chimney say to the other chimney?
  'I'm going out tonight — can I borrow your soot?'

What did one sardine say to the other sardine?
  'Move over — you're squashing me!'

What did one ear say to the other ear?
  'Just between us we need a haircut.'

What did the big bus say to the little bus?
  'You're too young to be driving.'

What did the big fly say to the little fly after they were both caught in a fly-paper?
  'This is a sticky problem!'

What did the woman with a bad cold say to the chemist?
  'I need a box of a-a-atishoos!'

What did one chick say to the other chick when it found an orange in their nest?
  'Look at the orange Mama laid!' (Orange Marmelade)

What did the little eye say to the big eye?
  'Aye, aye, Captain!'

What did one flea on Robinson Crusoe's knee say to the other flea on Robinson Crusoe's knee?
  'Bye for now — I'll see you on Friday!'

What did the toothpaste say to the toothbrush?
  'Give me a squeeze and I'll meet you outside the tube.'

Martini Hand
Is Frozen

Knock! Knock!

— Who's there?
Adolf.
Adolf who?
A dolf ball hid me in der moud and I can't dalk proper!

—Who's there?
Soup.
Soup who?
Soup-erman!

— Who's there?
Cows.
Cows who?
Cows go 'moo' not 'who'!

— Who's there?
Bet.
Bet who?
Bet you don't know who's knocking on your door!

— Who's there?
Juno.
Juno who?
Juno what the time is — my watch is broken?

— Who's there?
Europe.
Europe who?
Europe early this morning.

— Who's there?
Arfur.
Arfur who?
Arfur got.

— Who's there?
Egbert.
Egbert who?
Egbert no bacon.

— Who's there?
Luke. Luke who?
Luke through the keyhole and you'll see.

—Who's there?
Ken.
Ken who?
Ken I come in?

— Who's there?
Bella.
Bella who?
Bella not-a work so I knock-a on-a de door!

—Who's there?
Dismay.
Dismay who?
Dismay be a joke but it doesn't make me laugh!

— Who's there?
Toby.
Toby who?
Toby or not to be . . .

— Who's there?
Rupert.
Rupert who?
Rupert your left arm in, your left arm out . . .

— Who's there?
Dawn.
Dawn who?
Dawn leave me standing out here in the cold. *Or (Sing)*
'Dawn laugh at me 'cos I'm a fool . . .'

— Who's there?
Capfitz.
Capfitz who?
Capfitz you not who.

— Who's there?
Amos.
Amos who?
Amosquito.

— Who's there?
Anna.
Anna who?
Annather mosquito.

— Who's there?
Dishwasher.
Dishwasher who?
Dishwashn't de way I shpoke before I had falsh teeth!

— Who's there?
Martini.
Martini who?
Martini hand is frozen so let me in!

— Who's there?
Zephyr.
Zephyr who?
Zephyr de doctor, I got a code id de node.

— Who's there?
Owl.
Owl who?
Owl you know unless you open the door?

— Who's there?
Wendy.
Wendy who?
(Sing) Wendy red, red robin comes bob, bob, bobbin' along
. . .

— Who's there?
Sal.
Sal who?
(Sing) Sal-ong way to Tipperary . . .

—Who's there?
Phyllis.
Phyllis who?
Phyllis up with a glass of water — I'm parched.

— Who's there?
Aardvark.
Aardvark who?
(Sing) Aardvark a million miles for one of your smiles, My
Mammy . . .

— Who's there?
Doctor.
Doctor who?
Doctor Foster — I've just come from Gloucester.

— Who's there?
Arpo.
Arpo who?
Arpo ain't got no 'andle.

— Who's there?
Noah.
Noah who?
Noah good place to eat?

— Who's there?
Police.
Police who?
Police let me in — it's cold out here!

— Who's there?
Mickey.
Mickey who?
Mickey's stuck in the door!

— Who's there?
William.
William who?
William mind your own business!

— Who's there?
Mary.
Mary who?
Mary Christmas.

— Who's there?
One.
One who?
One-der why you keep asking that?

— Who's there?
Howard.
Howard who?
Howard you like to stand out here in the cold while some
idiot keeps saying 'Who's there . . . ?'

— Who's there?
Max.
Max who?
Max no difference — just open the door!

Law and Disorder

The police patrol-car driver was astounded to see, as he overtook a fast-moving car, that the woman at the wheel was knitting. He wound down his window and yelled, 'Pull over!' 'No,' she called back. 'A pair of socks!'

Seeing a woman standing helplessly by her car in a remote part of the countryside, the kindly policeman alighted from his bicycle and asked what was the matter. 'Oh, thank you, officer,' she said. 'I've had a flat tyre. I've managed to change the wheel, but now I can't lower the jack.' 'Very good, madam,' said the policeman. 'I'll see what I can do.' 'Please lower the car gently,' said the woman. 'My husband's asleep in the back seat!'

The policeman had brought a suspect in to the station and was smugly reporting his triumph to the sergeant.
   'Good work, Plod,' said the sergeant. 'Has he got a record?'
   'Oh, yes, Sarge,' said P.C. Plod. 'He's got three Adam Ants and a pile of Cliff Richard's . . .'

'I'll have to report you, sir,' said the traffic cop to the speeding driver. 'You were doing eighty-five miles an hour.' 'Nonsense, officer,' declared the driver. 'I've only been in the car for ten minutes!'

'Why were you speeding, madam?' asked the traffic cop.
   'Well, officer,' came the reply, 'my brakes are bad and I wanted to get home before I had an accident.'

'Last year I opened a jeweller's shop.'
   'Any good?'
   'No. He caught me at it.'

The only way a constable could quieten a rowdy drunk was to clonk him on the head with his truncheon. 'What was that?' said the drunk. 'It's just struck one,' said the policeman. 'Blimey!' said the drunk. 'It's a good thing I wasn't here an hour ago!'

'Last week in my self-service store a man served himself to three tins of peaches, the till and a pair of trousers!'
   'Didn't you chase after him?'
   'No — they were my trousers!'

'Stick 'em down!' snarled the fierce highwayman.
  'Eh?' said the startled passenger.
  'I said stick 'em down!'
  'Don't you mean stick 'em up?'
  'Oh — no wonder I'm losing money!'

Do you know what happened to the crook who stole the calendar? He get twelve months . . .

The criminal mastermind found one of his gang sawing the legs off his bed. 'What are you doing that for?' demanded the crook boss.
  'Only doing what you ordered,' said the stupid thug. 'You told me to lie low for a bit!'

Why did the police go to the chippy?
  'Cos they'd had a report of fish being battered.'

Why did the peanut complain to the police?
  'Cos he'd been assaulted.

'No trouble with the football fans this week, Sarge.'
  'Why's that, constable?'
  'United are playing away!'

'Now as I understand it, sir,' said the policeman to the motorist, 'you were driving this vehicle when the accident occurred. Can you tell me what happened?'
  'I'm afraid not, constable,' replied the motorist. 'I had my eyes shut!'

A crook dashed into a Chinese restaurant, brandished a sawn-off shot-gun under the manager's nose and said, 'I want everything you've got in the till!' To which the manager inscrutably replied, 'To take away?'

A murderer sitting in the electric chair was about to be executed. 'Have you any last request?' asked the prison chaplain.
  'Yes,' replied the wretched killer. 'Will you hold my hand?'

What do policemen in Hawaii say when they come across something suspicious? 'Aloha, aloha, aloha! What's going' on 'ere, then?!'

Policeman: 'Why are you driving with a bucket of water on the passenger seat?'
Motorist: 'So's I can dip my headlights!'

At three o'clock in the morning a policeman came across a suspicious character skulking down a side street carrying two suitcases. 'What's in the suitcase?' he demanded, pointing to one. 'That's sugar for my tea!' said the man. 'And what's in that suitcase?' asked the policeman, pointing to the other. 'That's sugar for my coffee!' replied the man, whereupon the policeman hit him on the head with his truncheon. 'What's that for?' said the man, rubbing his skull. 'That's a lump for your cocoa!'

A jeweller standing behind the counter of his shop was astounded to see a man come hurtling head-first through the window. 'What on earth are you up to?' he demanded. 'I'm terribly sorry,' said the man. 'I forgot to let go of the brick!'

Two petty crooks had been sent by the Big Boss to steal a van-load of goods from a bathroom suppliers. One stayed in the van as look-out and the other went into the storeroom. Fifteen minutes went by, then half an hour, then an hour — and no sign of him. The look-out crook finally grew impatient and went to look for his partner in crime. Inside the store the two came face to face.

'Where have you been?' demanded the worried look-out.

'The boss told me to take a bath,' came the reply, 'but I can't find the soap and towel!'

Lines for Loonies

Julius Caesar broke his beezer,
Playing squash with a lemon-squeezer!

Don't eat school dinners,
Just throw them aside.
A lot of kids didn't,
A lot of kids died.
The meat's made of iron,
The spuds are of steel,
And if *they don't* kill you,
The pudding will!

(To the tune of Frère Jacques)
School dinners! School dinners!
Concrete chips! Concrete chips!
Semolina pudding! Semolina pudding!
I feel sick — bathroom quick!

There was a young girl called Nelly,
Who was always watching the telly.
Her eyes grew square,
But she didn't care,
So they packed her off to Pwllheli.

(To the tune of My Darling Clementine)
Build a bonfire! Build a bonfire!
Put the teachers on the top;
Put the Headmaster in the middle,
Then burn the flippin' lot!

We go up and we go down,
We don't care if the school falls down;
No more English,
No more French,
No more sitting on the old school fence.
If the teacher interferes,
Tie her up and box her ears;
If that doesn't serve her right,
Blow her up with dynamite!

Row, row, row your boat,
Gently down the stream;
Throw the teacher overboard,
Then you'll hear her scream!

These are the graves of three poor sinners,
Who died after eating Grange School dinners.

Doctor Bell fell down the well,
And broke his collar-bone;
A doctor should attend the sick,
And leave the well alone!

There once was a great big cat,
Who swallowed a whole cricket bat;
He swallowed the ball,
The stumps, bails and all —
So the cricket team clobbered him flat!

Here come the bride,
Sixty inches wide;
Look at her now as she wobbles,
Up the centre aisle.
Here comes the groom,
Biting his nails in gloom,
He's looking as thin as a dressmaking pin,
And never again will he smile.

There once was an old man of Ealing,
Who had an expectorant feeling.
But a sign on the door,
Said DON'T SPIT ON THE FLOOR,
So he looked up and spat on the ceiling.

Little birdie flying high,
Dropped a message from the sky.
'Oh,' said the farmer wiping his eye,
'Isn't it lucky cows don't fly!'

I like my little school,
It's a nice little school,
It's built of bricks and plaster.
The only nasty thing,
In my nice little school,
Is the cross-eyed, bald-headed maths master!

Latin's a dead language,
As dead as dead can be;
It killed off all the Romans,
And now it's killing me!

*(The author's Latin master at school was
for some obscure reason known as Charlie,
which gave rise to the following ode —
substitute your own teacher's
name suitably Latinized.)*
Charlibus sittibus
On the deskinorum.
Deskibus collapsibus —
Charlie on the floorum!

Monkey Business

And Other Beastly Jokes

We call our dog Carpenter 'cos he's always doing little odd jobs around the house.

What happens when the frog's car breaks down?
  He gets toad away.

What is a crate of ducks?
  A box of quackers.

A mouse went into a music shop, jumped on to the counter and, to the astonishment of the owner, said 'Can I have a mouse-organ, please?'
  The music shop owner gulped and said, 'This is quite extraordinary. I've been here for thirty-five years and no mouse has ever asked for a mouse-organ until today — and you are the second! There was another mouse here just an hour or so ago, also asking for a mouse-organ.'
  'Ah yes,' said the mouse, 'That'll be 'Armonica . . .'

Why do cats and dogs turn round and round before sleeping?
  Because one good turn deserves another.

What do people in Mozambique call little black cats?
  Little black kittens.

What is a musical fish?
  A piano-tuna.

What does a frog do with bad eyesight?
  Hops to the hoptician.

Why are wolves like playing-cards?
  They both come in packs.

What birds hover over people lost in the desert?
  Luncheon vultures.

Why did the whale let Jonah go?
  He couldn't stomach him.

How can you get a set of teeth put in for free?
  Smack a tiger.

What did the goat say when he only had thistles to eat?
  'Thistle have to do.'

If a peacock lays an egg in your garden, who owns the egg?
  No one — peacocks don't lay eggs, only peahens.

How do you shoe a horse?
  Say 'Giddy-up!'

Where does a two-ton gorilla sit when he goes to the theatre?
  Anywhere he wants to!

'We had roast boar for dinner last night.'
  'Was it a wild boar?'
  'Well, it wasn't very pleased.'

Where do you find wild boar?
  Depends where you leave them.

What was the tortoise doing on the motorway?
  About 150 metres an hour.

What is the animal with the highest intelligence?
  A giraffe.

Why can't you trust an Indian leopard?
  'Cos it's a cheetah.

What happened at the badly organized milking contest?
  There was udder chaos.

Why was the camel unhappy?
  'Cos it had the hump.

Why are skunks always arguing?
  'Cos they like to raise a stink.

What animal are you like when you take a bath?
  A little bear.

If there are five partridges in a pear tree and a hunter shoots three, how many are left?
  None — the others flew away.

If twenty dogs run after one dog, what time is it?
  Twenty after one.

A man walked into a pub with a huge, vicious looking Alsatian. 'Sorry, sir,' said the landlord, 'but that dog looks dangerous to me. You'll have to leave him outside.' So the Alsatian owner took his dog outside, then came back into the bar and ordered a drink. He was just finishing when a young woman came in and said, 'Whose Alsatian is that outside?'

'Mine,' said its proud owner.

'I'm afraid,' said the young woman, 'that my dog's just killed him!'

'Killed him!' said the man in disbelief. 'What kind of dog do you have then?'

'A Chihuahua,' said the young woman.

'But how could a little Chihuahua kill my enormous Alsatian?'

'She got stuck in his throat and choked him.'

A woman bought two parrots, one of whom she was warned was extremely aggressive. And it was, too! When she took the cover off the cage the morning after bringing them home the aggressive parrot had killed the other stone dead! To teach it a lesson she then bought a condor — and again when she took the cover off the cage the next morning the parrot had put paid to the intruder. Determined not to be beaten the woman then bought an eagle! In the morning she took the cover off — and there was the eagle, dead on the floor of the cage! But this time the parrot was completely denuded of feathers! It stood on its perch, totally featherless, cocked its head on one side, looked at its mistress and said, 'I really had to take my coat off to that one!'

Why can't you play jokes on snakes?
'Cos you can never pull their legs.

A man standing at a bus-stop was eating fish and chips. Next to him stood a lady with her little dog, which became very excited at the smell of the man's supper and began whining and jumping up at him. 'Do you mind if I throw him a bit?' said the man to the lady. 'No, not at all,' she replied. Whereupon the man picked up the dog and threw him over a wall . . .

Which shop do sheep like to visit?
The baaaber's!

What's worse than a crocodile with tooth-ache?
A centipede with bunions.

What's the definition of a caterpillar?
A worm with a fur coat.

The loud-mouthed frog said to the giraffe, 'What do you eat, Mr Giraffe?' 'Leaves,' said the giraffe. The loud-mouthed frog then said to the antelope, 'And what do you eat, Mr Antelope?' 'Grass,' said the antelope. So the loud-mouthed frog then said to the crocodile, 'And what do you eat, Mr Crocodile?' 'Loud-mouthed frogs,' said the crocodile, to which the loud-mouthed frog replied, *(with your mouth tightly shut)* 'Oh, you don't get many of those round here!'

Why do bees hum?
  'Cos they don't know the words.

A man buying a camel was advised that to make it walk he should say 'Few!', to make it run he should say 'Many!', and to make it stop he should say 'Amen!' At his first ride all went well. 'Few!' he called, and off the camel went. 'Many!' he shouted, and the camel began to run — straight for the edge of a cliff. But the new owner had forgotten the word to make the camel stop! As the cliff edge came closer and closer he called out in terror, 'Lord save me! Lord save me! Amen!' And of course the camel stopped — right on the very edge of the precipice. Whereupon the rider mopped his brow in relief and said, 'Phew, that was clo-AAAAGH!''

Two fish were swimming in a stream when it began to rain. 'Quick!' said one fish to the other, 'Let's swim under that bridge, otherwise we'll get wet!''

What animal is like a nursery rhyme?
  Ee, Aw, Marjorie Daw . . .!

A family of tortoises went into a cafe for some ice-cream. They sat down and were about to start when Father Tortoise said, 'I think it's going to rain. Junior, will you pop home and fetch my umbrella?' So off went Junior Tortoise for his father's umbrella, but three days later he still hadn't returned. 'I think, dear,' said Mother Tortoise to Father Tortoise, 'we'd better eat Junior's ice-cream before it melts.' And a voice from the door said, 'If you do that I won't go!'

What does a cat turn into when the lights go out?
  The dark.

'Who's been eating my porridge?' squeaked Baby Bear.
'Who's been eating *my* porridge?' growled Father Bear.
'Don't get all excited,' said Mother Bear. 'I haven't made it yet!'

'Who's been eating my porridge?' squeaked Baby Bear.
'Who's been eating *my* porridge?' cried Mother Bear.
'Burp!' said Father Bear . . .

'My dog died of 'flu.'
'But dogs don't get 'flu.'
'Mine flew under a bus.'

Which animal goes to sleep with its shoes on?
  A horse.

If a farmer stands in a field with his dog and forty pigs, how many feet have they got between them? Two — only the farmer has feet!

Oh, No!

What did Lot do when his wife turned into a pillar of salt?
He put her in the cellar.

What kind of lights did Noah have on the ark?
Floodlights.

Why do actors hang around snooker halls?
'Cos that's where they are sure to get some cues.

What kind of umbrella does a Russian carry when its raining?
A wet one!

Why was the baby raised on cat's milk?
'Cos it was a baby kitten.

What is yellow, soft and goes round and round?
A long-playing omelette.

What is the shortest bridge in the world?
The bridge of your nose.

What do you call an Irish spider?
Paddy Longlegs.

What did the French Chef do when a customer fainted?
Gave her the quiche of life.

Is censorship a good thing or not?
It depends on whether the result makes censor not.

When are circus acrobats needed in restaurants?
When tumblers are required on the tables.

If we get honey from a bee, what do we get from a wasp?
Waspberry jam.

Who sailed the Seven Seas looking for rubbish and blubber?
Binbag the Whaler.

Why did the scientist have his phone cut off?
  'Cos he wanted to win the Nobel prize.

Why is the Eiffel tower so called?
  'Cos from the top you sure get an eye-ful!

What would you say to a German barber?
  'Good morning, Herr Dresser!'

Why was Cleopatra so cantankerous?
  She was Queen of denial.

What is the definition of a minimum?
  A woman with only one child.

What food is impertinent?
  Sauce.

What is a cow that eats grass?
  A lawn-mooer.

What is purple and 4,000 miles long?
  The Grape Wall of China.

Why did the Lone Ranger take a hammer to bed?
  So's he could hit the hay.

Who was Mexico's most famous fat man?
  Pauncho Villa.

What will happen to you at Christmas?
  Yule be happy.

What clothes do lawyers wear in court?
  Lawsuits.

What's rich and goes putt-putt?
  A sunburned golf-pro.

What is big, has four wheels and flies?
  A rubbish cart.

Why did the antelope?
  Nobody gnu.

Why should Elijah's parents be remembered by all business people?
Because they made a prophet.

Why did the father call two of his sons Edward?
'Cos two Eds are better than one.

What do you call someone who steals pigs?
A ham-burglar.

What did Queen Guinevere say when she fell in love?
'Arthur any more at home like you?'

Did Cain hate his brother for ever?
No, just for as long as he was Abel.

What is black and white and has eight wheels?
A nun on roller skates.

Where were chips first fried?
In Greece.

What soup do Irish cannibals like best?
The broth of a boy.

How did the glow-worm feel when it backed into a fan?
Delighted.

What did the guests sing at the Eskimo's coming-of-age party?
'Freeze A Jolly Good Fellow . . .'

What is the definition of 'debate'?
It's something dat lures de fish.

What is Shakespeare's most popular play in the Orient?
Asia Like It.

What will a wise man say on the Last Day?
'Armageddon out of here . . .'

What is yellow and goes click-click?
A ball-point banana.

What is Father Christmas's wife called?
Mrs Christmas.

What did Mrs Christmas say to her husband during the storm?
'Come and look at the reindeer.'

Do sailors go on safaris?
  Not safaris I know.

What drink do jungle big cats prefer?
  Lyons quick brew.

What's big, hairy and can fly?
  King Kongcorde.

What has a horn and drives?
  A car.

What lives in a pod and is a Kung Fu expert?
  Bruce Pea.

Why are you tired on April Fool's Day?
  'Cos you've just had a thirty-one days' March.

Why are adults boring?
  'Cos they're groan-ups.

What do cannibal children like playing best?
  Swallow my leader.

What do Eskimos use for money?
  Ice lolly.

What kind of warmth do sheep enjoy in winter?
  Central bleating.

Why did Henry VIII have so many wives?
  He liked to chop and change.

What kinds of cans are there in Mexico?
  Mexicans.

How would you define a stick of rhubarb?
  A stick of celery with high blood-pressure.

Why did the fireman wear red trousers?
  His blue ones were at the cleaners.

Why are goldfish gold?
  So they won't go rusty.

What is a mermaid?
  A deep-she fish.

'Why are you taking that steel wool home?'
'I'm going to knit myself a car.'

Did you hear about the stupid water-polo player?
His horse drowned . . .

Did you hear the joke about the roof?
It's way above your head.

What happened to the idiot who sat on the floor?
She fell off.

Did you hear about the stupid tap-dancer?
He fell in the sink.

Why did the bald-headed man look out of the window?
To get some fresh 'air.

Where does Tarzan buy his clothes?
At a Jungle Sale.

What did Tarzan say when the tiger started chewing on his leg?
AAAAAAAAAAAAAAAAA! (Give Tarzan yell)

Why did the orange stop rolling down the hill?
It ran out of juice.

How can you put on weight easily?
Eat an entire peach and you'll immediately gain a stone.

Who makes suits and eats spinach?
Popeye the Tailorman.

Why couldn't Cinderella go to the ball?
'Cos it had a puncture.

Preserve wild-life — pickle a squirrel.

What is the crocodile's favourite game?
Snap.

If King Kong went to Hong Kong to play ping-pong and died, what would they put on his coffin?
A lid.

When a lemon calls for assistance, what does it want?
Lemonade.

If you drop a white hat into the Red Sea, how does it come out?
   Wet.

What's green and white and bounces?
   A spring onion.

How do you make gold soup?
   Use fourteen carats.

Where do bees go for transport?
   The buzz-stop.

What's white and climbs trees?
   A fridge — I lied about it climbing trees.

What's white and blue and climbs trees?
   A fridge wearing denims. (And I'm still lying about it climbing trees.)

What vegetable plays snooker?
   A cue-cumber.

How do pixies eat?
   By gobblin'.

How do you cut through the waves?
   With a sea-saw.

Do robots have brothers?
   No, only tran*sisters*.

Why do some women wear curlers at night?
   So they can wake up curly in the morning.

What pop group kills household germs?
   The Bleach Boys.

What do miners play in the pit?
   Mine-opoly.

What's yellow and goes round and round?
   A banana in a washing machine.

What happened to the man who dreamed he was eating a giant marshmallow?
   When he woke up his pillow had disappeared.

What happened to the man who slept with his head under the pillow?
When he woke up he found the fairies had taken all his teeth out.

What do you call a potato that insults the farmer?
A fresh vegetable.

Why couldn't the sailors play cards?
'Cos the captain was standing on the deck.

What's black and white and extremely difficult?
An A-level exam paper.

What did the policeman have in his sandwiches?
Traffic jam.

Why did the cockerel cross the road?
To show he wasn't chicken.

How do you take a sick pig to hospital?
In a hambulance.

Where do you take a sick dog?
To the dogtor.

What do you get if you give sugar and egg-whites to a monkey?
Meringue Outan.

What does a pig use to write his letters with?
Pen and oink.

We all know that a nun rolling down a hill goes black-and-white-and-black-and-white, but what is black-and-white and goes ha-ha? The nun that pushed her!

What was Beethoven's favourite fruit? (Sing to the opening four notes of Beethoven's Fifth Symphony:)
Banana-*naaaa!*

Have you heard the joke about the dog that walked twice from Land's End to John O'Groats?
No, neither have I . . .

What's a good place for water-skiing?
A sloping lake.

Where would you find a stupid shop-lifter?
Squashed under Tesco's.

Who invented fire?
  Some bright spark . . .

If you put a crowd of Mastermind contestants in a London Underground train, what have you got?
  A Tube of Smarties.

What fish are other fish most scared of?
  Jack the Kipper.

What would you call a goods train loaded with sweets?
  A Chew-Chew train.

What comes out of a wardrobe at one hundred miles an hour?
  Stirling Moth.

What goes 'Click-click — have I done it?'
  A blind man doing the Rubik Cube.

What jacket is always burning?
  A blazer.

What makes a tree noisy?
  Its bark.

What is black and swings through trees?
  Tarzan's coalman.

Why is a bee's hair always sticky?
  'Cos it uses a honeycomb.

What fruit starts with the letter N?
  A 'nana.

What do you get if you drop a piano on an army camp?
  A flat major.

What happened to the hyena who swallowed an Oxo cube?
  He made a laughing stock of himself.

What do frogs drink?
  Croaka Cola.

Where would you weigh a pie?
  (Sing) Somewhere over the rainbow, weigh a pie . . .
(way up high!)

Who is in cowboy films and is always broke?
  Skint Eastwood.

Why didn't the banana snore?
  'Cos it was afraid to wake up the rest of the bunch.

What looks like half a loaf of bread?
  The other half.

Who is the biggest gangster in the sea?
  Al Caprawn.

What pantomime story is set in a chemist's shop?
  Puss in Boots.

What do you call ants who run away very fast to get married?
  Ant-elopers.

What does Luke Skywalker shave with?
  A laser blade.

Did you hear about the idiot who had a brain transplant?
  The brain rejected him!

Why do so many Irish people emigrate?
  Because MacGillicuddy Reeks!

Why did the idiot have his sundial floodlit?
  So's he could tell the time at night.

How do you cope with a gas leak?
  Put a bucket under it.

If you want to know where the sun goes after it has set, just stay up all night and it will finally dawn on you!

What's yellow and leaps from cake to cake?
  Tarzipan.

What's the fastest thing in water?
  A motor-pike.

Hear about the world's worst athlete? He ran a bath and came in second.

What's very intelligent and loves boating?
  A row-bot.

Where do snowmen go to dance?
  A snowball.

How did the Mother Babana spoil the Baby Banana?
  She left him in the sun too long.

Which capital city cheats at exams?
  Peking.

What do you call a flea that lives in an idiot's ear?
  A space invader.

Why did the woman take a load of hay to bed?
  To feed her nightmare.

What is Kojak's favourite washing powder?
  Bald Automatic.

What do cats prefer for breakfast?
  Mice Crispies.

What do ants take when they are ill?
  Antibiotics.

Where do astronauts park their space vehicles?
  On meet-eorites.

What's furry and minty?
  A Polo bear.

What's black and white and noisy?
  A zebra with a drum-kit.

What's red, has wheels, and lies on its back?
  A dead bus.

What's yellow and goes slam-slam-slam-slam?
  A four-door banana.

Why did the idiot jump out of the window?
  To try out his new spring suit.

Why did the idiot spring out of the window?
  To try out his new jump suit.

Did you hear about the Irish Kamikaze pilot?
  He flew ninety-nine missions . . .

Did you hear about the idiot Morris dancer?
  He fell off the bonnet.

How do you kill an Aberdonian?
  Throw a 5p piece under a bus.

Did you hear about the terrorist who tried to blow up a bus?
  He burnt his lips on the exhaust pipe.

What's black and white and bounces?
  A penguin on a pogo-stick. *Or* An india-rubber nun.

What do you call a sleeping heifer?
  A young bulldozer.

Shall I tell you the joke about the postcard that hadn't been
stamped? No, you'd never get it.

What pipes are never played in Scotland?
  Hose-pipes.

The Old Jokes at Home

'*Why is your brother called Flannel?*'
  'Cos he shrinks from washing!'

One little boy's family were so poor they used sugar sacks for nappies. He had to take the rough with the smooth. He was ten before he realized his name wasn't Tate & Lyle...

'*Any luck with your advertisement for a husband?*'
  'Yes, I've had sixteen replies. And they all say the same thing.'
  'What's that?'
'You can have mine!'
  'You can have mine!'

Why did the comedian's wife sue him for divorce?
  He kept trying to joke her to death.

'My Dad's in hospital. Last week he went down the garden to cut a cabbage for our dinner. The knife slipped and he stabbed himself.'
  'Gosh! What did your Mum do?
  'Opened up a tin of peas.'

'Mummy, may I leave the table?'
  'Well, you certainly can't take it with you!'

Despite his big brother's warnings, little Jasper insisted on walking along the top of a high wall. 'Well,' said big brother, 'if you fall and break both your legs, don't come running to me!'

'Daddy, I don't like cheese with holes.'
  'Just eat the cheese and leave the holes on the side of your plate.'

'Grandma, what's a weapon?'
  'A weapon is something you fight with.'
  'You mean like Grandad?'

59

'Kevin,' said little Ernie to his big brother, 'what does that big L on the car mean?'

'It means I'm learning to drive,' said Kevin.

A few weeks later Kevin had passed his test and was preparing to take his car to France; to the rear of the car he affixed the customary GB sticker.

'Kevin,' said little Ernie, 'does GB mean you're getting better?'

Sandra and Simon were arguing furiously over the breakfast table. 'Oh, you're stupid!' shouted Simon. 'Simon!' said their father, 'that's quite enough of that! Now, say you're sorry.'

'All right,' said Simon. 'Sandra, I'm sorry you're stupid.'

'Is your brother fat?'

I'll say! He's so fat he had mumps for three weeks before we found out!'

'How was it you were born in Sheffield?

' 'Cos my mother wanted me near her.'

Why was the Egyptian girl worried?
'Cos her Daddy was a Mummy.

Why did Grandpa put wheels on his rocking-chair?
'Cos he wanted to Rock'n'Roll.

'Katie, have you finished your alphabet soup?'
'Not yet, Mum. I'm only up to the Ks . . .'

Little Helen and her Mummy were in the cinema. After half an hour or so of the main feature, Helen whispered 'Mummy, is your seat comfortable?' 'Yes, thank you, dear,' replied her mother. 'Can you see the screen all right?' 'Yes, thank you, dear.' 'Are you sitting in a draught?' 'No, dear.' 'Then can I swap places with you?'

'Mummy, I don't want to go to France!'
'Shut up and start swimming . . .'

'Mummy, why can't we have a dustbin like everyone else?'
'Shut up and keep eating.'

The family seated in a restaurant had finished their dinners when Father called over the waiter. 'Yes, sir?' said the waiter.

'My son has left quite a lot of meat on his plate,' explained Father. 'Could you give me a bag so that I can take it home for the dog?'

'Gosh, Dad!' exclaimed the excited boy. 'Have we got a dog then?'

Did you hear about the three daughters in the kitchen?
    One washed up, one dried up, and the third picked up the pieces.

'Mrs Finnegan!' said her neighbour crossly, 'Have you told your son to stop imitating me?'
    'Yes, I've told him to stop acting the fool!'

'Stephen, it's time for your violin lesson.'
    'Oh, fiddle!'

'Stephen, it's time for your drum lesson.'
    'Oh, smashing!'

Little brother: 'Look, Sis, I've got a pack of cards.'
Big sister: 'Big deal!'

Father: 'Well, Susie, did you have a good time at school today?'
Susie: 'Only home time!'

For her tenth birthday Jessica received a bottle of perfume and a recorder. For supper that evening were two old friends of her parents, and as she sat between them at table she confided, 'If you hear a little noise and smell a little smell — it's me!'

'Steve, you've been fighting again, haven't you?'
    'Yes, Mum.'
    'You must try and control your temper. Didn't I tell you to count up to 10?'
    'Yes, but Vic's Mum only told him to count up to five so he hit me first!'

Amos asked his mother whether they could have a video.
    'I'm afraid we can't afford one,' sighed his mother.
    But on the following day in came Amos, staggering beneath the weight of a brand-new video.
    'How on earth did you pay for that?' gasped his mother.
    'Easy, Mum,' replied Amos. 'I sold the television!'

Why did Henry put a frog in his sister's bed?
    ''Cos he couldn't catch a mouse.

A Yorkshire man whose wife died instructed the stonemason to carve on her headstone the words 'She Was Thine'. But when he went to inspect the result the mason had put 'She Was Thin'. The grieving widower angrily informed the artisan that he had left an E out. 'Sorry,' said the stonemason, 'Ah'll put it reet for thee, never fear. A'll put t'E in tomorrow.' But when the widower went to see the tombstone the legend now read, 'E, She Was Thin . . .'

And do you like your new school?' asked grandmother fondly.

'Well, sometimes, Granny,' said little Jacob.

'And what times are those?'

'When it's shut!'

'What does your Dad do?'

'He's a Government artist.'

'What does he draw?'

'The dole!'

Pix 'n' Posers

What's this?

Fifteen Mexicans walking down a mountain path.

How can one plus one equal a window?

 Put these together and you get

What's this?

A koala climbing up a tree.

What's this?

A Mexican riding a bicycle.

What's this?

A fountain-pen nib.

Put down ten matches to make the word WET. How can you remove two matches yet still have a three-letter word? You simply remove the first two matches, leaving the word VET!

Before WET   After VET

Say to a friend: Do you know Shakespeare's stamp? *Your friend will say 'No' and you then say* Shake . . . *(shaking him by the shoulders)* . . . spear . . . *(spearing him)* . . . stamp! *(Stamping on his toe!)*

If it takes ten men four days to dig a hole, how long will it take five men to dig half a hole? There's no such thing as half a hole!

A boy wanted to cross a river from south to north; he couldn't swim, no boats were available, and the only bridge was watched over by a guard who came out of his hut every five minutes. As it took ten minutes to walk across the bridge how did the boy achieve his goal?
Answer: He walked across from south to north; as the guard emerged from his hut the boy turned round and pretended he was walking from north to south. The guard then ran after him and shooed the boy back the way he thought he had come — i.e. to the north side of the river!

How can a cock lay an egg on barbed wire?
Cocks don't lay eggs, only hens!

If a man rides into an inn on Friday and stays three days, how can he ride out on Friday?
Answer: Friday was the name of his horse!

A donkey wanted to cross a stream in order to eat the lush grass in the meadow opposite. There was no bridge, no boat, and the donkey couldn't swim. So how did he cross? . . . You give up? . . . So did the donkey!

Three boys called Peter, Paul and Pardon went to play by the river. Peter and Paul fell in and were drowned: who was left? *(You will of course receive the reply 'Pardon', at which you repeat loudly:)* Three boys called Peter, Paul and Pardon . . . etc.

A motorist in his car with his two sons was involved in a collision. He and one of his sons were killed outright, and the other son was taken to hospital, where the doctor said, 'This is my son.' How can this be?
Answer: The doctor was his mother.

In the school the backward children were placed in a classroom on the ground floor, the stupid children on the first floor, the naughty children on the second floor, and the really thick tearaways on the third floor. What was on the top floor? The teachers' staff-room!

A frog is lying on a lilypad in the middle of a pond. If he is six inches from the north edge, six inches from the south edge, and four inches from the east and west edges, in which direction will he jump to get out of the pond?

He won't jump at all because he's dead.

I saw Esau sitting on a see-saw — how many S's in that?

There aren't any S's in THAT!

A man with a cat, a mouse and a lump of cheese has to cross a river in a small boat, but he can only take one thing with him at a time. So how does he get them all across without the cat eating the mouse or the mouse eating the cheese?
Answer: First he crosses with the mouse, then he crosses with the cat and returns *with the mouse* which he leaves behind while he crosses with the cheese, finally returning for the mouse!

If a red house had red bricks, a blue house has blue bricks, a black house has black bricks and a pink house has pink bricks, what colour bricks does a green house have? A greenhouse doesn't have bricks — only glass!

A diesel train enters a tunnel running due north-south. If the train enters the tunnel at the north end, which way does the smoke blow?

Diesel trains don't have smoke!

'What's five Q and five Q?'
'Ten Q.'
'You're welcome!'

A man is in a prison cell with no doors and no windows; there are no holes in the ceiling or trapdoors in the floor, yet in the morning the warders find him gone. How did he get out?
Answer: Through the door*way* — there were no doors, remember?!

Is it 'nine and five *is* thirteen' or 'nine and five *are* thirteen'?
Neither — nine and five are fourteen!

What was the tallest mountain in the world before Mount Everest was discovered?
Answer: Still Mount Everest — the fact that it was un-discovered makes no difference, it was still the highest mountain in the world.

If a dog is tied to a rope fifteen feet long, how can it reach a bone thirty feet away?
Answer: The rope isn't tied to anything!

How can you drop an egg three feet on to a concrete path without breaking it?
Answer: Drop it *four* feet. It will certainly be smashed, but only after dropping *more* than three feet!

'Did you hear about the fool who keeps going round saying No?'
'No.'
'Oh, so it's you!'

In an apple-eating contest Sue ate ninety apples and Selena ate a hundred and one. How many more apples did Selena eat than Sue?
Answer: Ten — Selena ate a hundred and *won!*

Say to a pal 'What's this?' Then wave your hand in a snake-like motion. Your pal will say 'I don't know', so then you wave your other hand in a similar manner and say 'Nor do I — but here comes another one!'

A man committed suicide by hanging himself from a high beam in a remote barn. There was no way to climb up to the beam, and the only thing the police found in the barn was a puddle of water beneath the body. How did he get up to the beam in order to hang himself?
Answer: He stood on a block of ice!

A deaf and dumb man went into an ironmonger's shop to buy a hammer. He couldn't speak so he mimed hammering... then another deaf and dumb man went in wanting a screwdriver, so he mimed putting in a screw... Then a blind man went into the shop and he wanted a saw. So what sort of mime did he do?
He didn't mime at all — he just asked for it!

Two boys were born on the same day, on the same date, to the same set of parents. They look alike, talk alike, think alike and behave alike — yet they are not twins! How can this be?
Answer: Because they are two of a set of triplets!

Try this on a friend. Ask 'Would you kiss a tramp for £1?' The answer will of course be 'No!' Then you ask 'Would you kiss a tramp for £5?' And again the answer will be 'No!' You then ask 'Would you kiss a tramp for £10?' And for the third time the answer will be in the negative. But then you say, 'What would you kiss a tramp for?' The answer you receive this time will probably be, 'Nothing.' To which you reply, 'Oh, so you'd kiss a tramp for nothing, would you?!' Or the reply might be, 'I wouldn't kiss a tramp for anything!' to which you can respond, 'So you would kiss a tramp for something, then!'

'Why doesn't the Queen wave with this hand?' (*Wave your left hand*)
'I don't know. Why?'
'Because it's *my* hand!'

'Let's have a race to say the alphabet.'
'All right.'
'The alphabet — beat you!'

As I was going to St Ives,
I met a man with seven wives.
Every wife had seven sacks,
Every sack had seven cats.
Every cat had seven kits —
Kits, cats, sacks, wives,
How many were going to St Ives?
Answer: Only me — all the rest were coming *from* St Ives!

'Which would you rather be—half-drowned or saved?'
  'Saved, of course.'
  'But if you're only half-drowned you *are* saved!'

A tropical lily is growing in a pond. If it doubles its size every day and takes twenty-two days to fill the entire area of the pond, how far will it have reached on the twenty-first day?
Answer: Half-way — because it doubles its size every day!

What is frozen water? Ice.
What is frozen cream? Ice-cream.
What is frozen tea? Iced tea.
What is frozen coffee? Iced coffee.
What is frozen ink? Iced ink. (I stink).
You'd better go and have a bath, then!

'You still owe me twenty pence for that honey.'
  'What honey?'
  'I never knew you cared!'

If there are fifty-two weeks in the year how many seconds are there?
Twelve — January 2nd, February 2nd, March 2nd, etc., etc.

Which month in the year has twenty-eight days? All of them...

What's your favourite colour? Red? And what is your favourite animal? A cat? And what is your favourite number? Seven? So when did you last see a red cat with seven legs...?!

If you have an umpire in cricket and a referee in football, what do you have in bowls?
  Goldfish.

If an aeroplane crashed on the borders of England and Scotland, where would the survivors be buried?
  Nowhere, 'cos any survivors wouldn't be dead!

Riddle-Tee-Hee

Why are 4,840 square yards like a bad tooth?
   Because it's an acre.

What is bought by the yard and worn by the foot?
   A carpet.

Why did the apple turnover?
   'Cos it saw the cheese roll.

If a runner gets athlete's foot, what does a Roman Catholic priest get?
   Mistletoe. (Missal-toe!)

Why does a Scoutmaster have to take a lot of rubbish?
   Because he's a Skip.

What cakes do children dislike?
   Cakes of soap.

Why is it dangerous to put the letter 'M' into the fridge?
   Because it changes ice into mice.

Why is the sea always restless?
   'Cos it's got so many rocks in its bed.

What did one toe say to the next toe?
   Don't look now but there's a big heel following us!

Why are your tonsils unhappy?
   'Cos they're always down in the mouth.

When is a schoolkid like a rope?
   When it's taut.

What's the best place to go to when you're dying?
   The living room.

How many coats can you get in an empty wardrobe?
   Only one — after that it isn't empty!

Why are whist players aggressive?
  'Cos they often lead with a club.

Where do you get satisfaction from?
  A satisfactory.

What question always receives the answer Yes?
  How do you pronounce Y E S?

Why did the milkmaid sit down?
  'Cos she couldn't stand milking.

Who is bigger: Mrs Bigger or her baby?
  Her baby, who is always a Little Bigger.

Why does a young lady need the letter Y?
  'Cos without it she'd be a young lad.

How does a ship listen?
  Through its engineers.

What do you have when you don't feel well?
  Gloves on your hands.

Who earns a living without doing a day's work?
  A night-porter.

How can you always tell an undertaker?
  By his grave manner.

Why is your nose in the middle of your face?
  'Cos it's the (s)centre.

Why is the sea so suspicious?
  'Cos it's been crossed so often.

Why did the train go 'ouch!'?
  'Cos it had a tender behind.

How many balls of string would it take to reach the Moon?
  Just one *HUGE* one!

What is it that even the most careful person overlooks?
  His nose.

On which side of Jack Trot's house did his Beanstalk grow?
  On the outside.

What goes up a chimney down but not down a chimney up?
  An umbrella.

What did the digital watch say to her mother?
    'Look, Ma! No hands!'

Why are there so few lady pilots?
    'Cos no girl wants to be a plane woman!

Why is perfume always very obedient?
    'Cos it is scent wherever it goes.

Why can the world never come to an end?
    'Cos it's round.

Why is Buckingham Palace cheap to maintain?
    'Cos it's run for a sovereign.

Why is the letter A like noon?
    'Cos it's in the middle of the day.

Why is an airplane like a confidence trickster?
    They both have no visible means of support.

What happened to the man who jumped off a bridge in Paris?
    He went in Seine.

Why did the weeping willow weep?
    'Cos it saw the pine tree pine.

How do barbers get to their shops quickly?
    They take short cuts.

Why are dentists unhappy?
    'Cos they're always looking down in the mouth.

Why can't a car play football?
    'Cos it's only got one boot.

Which word is always pronounced wrongly?
    The one that's spelled W R O N G L Y.

Why is the letter T an island?
    'Cos it's in the middle of water.

When were there only three vowels in the alphabet?
    Before U and I were born.

Why is the letter A like a flower?
    'Cos B is always after it.

Why did the Communist chicken cross the road?
  'Cos it was a Rhode Island Red.

What pet makes the loudest noise?
  A trum-pet.

What do you always take down when you're run over by a car?
  Its registration number.

Why did the hedgehog cross the road?
  To see his flatmate.

Why did the cat cross the road?
  'Cos it was stapled to the chicken . . . (ugh!)

Where was Rosie when the lights went out?
  In the dark.

What key went to University?
  A Yale.

What flashes by but doesn't move?
  A telegraph pole when you're travelling in a car.

Why was the Boy Scout dizzy?
  He'd done too many good turns.

What tune do you sing in a car?
  A car-toon.

What is full of holes but can hold water?
  A sponge.

What did the bell say when it fell in the water?
  'I'm (w)ringing wet!'

What makes the Tower of Pisa lean?
  It doesn't eat much.

Why are bakers invariably good people?
  'Cos they earn an honest crust.

Why did the bus stop?
'Cos it saw the zebra crossing.

Why did the pop singer go to the barber?
  He couldn't stand his hair any longer.

How do you get rid of varnish?
  Take away the letter R.

What athlete is the warmest in winter?
  The long jumper.

Which roof covers the noisiest tenant?
  The roof of your mouth.

What doesn't ask questions but must always be answered?
  A telephone.

What fish do dogs chase?
  Catfish.

What is open when it's closed and closed when it's open?
  Tower Bridge.

If a crocodile makes shoes what does a banana make?
  Slippers.

What travels faster: heat or cold?
  Heat, because it's easy to catch a cold.

What travels round the world yet stays in one corner?
  A postage stamp.

What two kinds of fish are needed to make a shoe?
  A sole and an eel.

Did you hear about the red sauce chasing the brown sauce?
  It couldn't ketchup.

How many days of the week start with the letter T?
  Four: Tuesday, Thursday, today and tomorrow.

What is a tornado?
  Mother Nature doing the twist.

What do you call a letter when it's dropped down the chimney?
  Blackmail.

Why is a chemistry lesson like a worm in a cornfield?
  They both go in one ear and out the other.

What runs and whistles but can't talk?
  A railway train.

What jam can't you put on your bread?
  Traffic jam.

What nail can't you hit with a hammer?
  Your fingernail.

'Look, there's a nail!'
  'Where?'
  'On the end of my finger!'

What driver can't drive?
  A screwdriver.

What vegetable do you need a plumber for?
  A leek!

Where can you find ice-cream in the Bible?
  At the Walls of Jericho.

Have you heard the joke about the wall?
  You'd never get over it!

What's the biggest nut in the British Army?
  The kernel.

Why did the rabbit cross the road?
  To show his girl-friend he had guts.

Why is a lion in the desert like Christmas?
  'Cos of its Sandy Claws.

What happens if you walk under a cow?
  You get a pat on the head.

What are the best things to put in an apple pie?
  Your teeth!

What has four eyes and a mouth?
  The Mississippi.

What gets bigger the more you take away?
  A hole.

What whistles when it's hot?
  A kettle.

What is a sausage dog?
  A hot dog with no bread.

How would you describe beans on toast?
  Skinheads on a raft.

What is the longest word in the dictionary?
  Elastic, because it stretches.

What runs round a garden without moving?
  A fence.

How does an octopus go into battle?
  Fully-armed.

Why did King Kong climb up the Empire State Building?
  To catch a plane.

What do you find in Quality Street?
  Chocolates.

What is the principal part of a lion?
  Its mane.

What should you do if your nose goes on strike?
  Picket.

Who won the World Cup in 1920?
  No one — the first World Cup competition was held in 1930.

What is the best place for a party on board ship?
  Where the funnel be.

What is the softest bed a baby can sleep on?
  Cot-on wool.

A barrel of beer fell on a brewery worker. Why wasn't he hurt?
  'Cos it was full of light ale.

Why is a batsman a coward?
  'Cos he's frightened of a duck.

What am I if someone takes away all my letters?
  A postman who's been mugged.

How can you avoid falling hair?
  Jump out of the way.

How can you knock over a full glass without spilling any water?
  Knock over a full glass of milk.

What can never be made right?
Your left ear.

What can you make that can't be seen?
A noise.

What is the best way to cover a cushion?
Sit on it.

If twelve make a dozen how many make a million?
Very few.

What do misers do when it's cold?
Sit round a candle.
What do misers do when it's very cold?
Light it.

What did the idiot do with a flea in his ear?
He shot it.

What is a container that hasn't any hinges but inside has a golden treasure?
An egg.

A little thing, a pretty thing, without a top or bottom. What am I?
A diamond ring.

What is the fastest vegetable in the world?
A runner bean!

What did the man say when he stepped on a choc bar?
'I've set foot on Mars!'

What bow can't you tie?
A rainbow.

What is the hottest part of the Sun?
Page three!

How does a professional hypnotist travel?
By public transport.

What is the smallest ant in the world?
An infant.

What is always behind time?
The back of a clock.

Why should you always have plenty of clocks in the house?
Because time is precious.

Why did the simpleton bury his car battery?
  'Cos the mechanic told him it was dead.

What do you get in Friday papers?
  Fish and chips. (Fri-day)

Why did the stupid postman get the sack?
  To put his stupid letters in.

Why was the United Nations worried when a waiter dropped his tray?
  'Cos it was the fall of Turkey, China was broken and Greece was overthrown!

Rolling in the Aisles

Vicar, come quickly! The church is on fire!'
  'Holy smoke!'

One Sunday the vicar concluded his sermon by saying, 'The preacher for next Sunday will be hung in the porch . . .!'

'Don't you enjoy the sound of church bells?'
  'Sorry?'
  'I said "don't you like the bells?" '
  'Eh?'
  'AREN'T THE BELLS WONDERFUL?'
  'It's no good — I can't hear a word you're saying for those blooming bells!'

Sunday School teacher: 'Who sits at the right hand of God?'
Sunday School pupil: 'Er — Mrs God?'

'I didn't see you in church last Sunday, Nigel. I hear you were out playing football instead.'
  'That's not true, vicar. And I've got the fish to prove it.'

Jemima had just returned from her first visit to Sunday School.
  'Well, Jemima,' asked her father, 'did you learn much?'
  'Not a lot,' said the little one. 'I've got to go back next week.'

Young Oliver had heard a sermon in which the preacher, when talking about Man's origins and ultimate destiny, had used the Biblical phrase 'Ashes to ashes, dust to dust'. Oliver returned home and went up to his room; but a few minutes later he came running downstairs and yelled to his mother, 'Mum — you'd better come upstairs!'
  'Why, Oliver?'
  ' 'Cos I just looked under my bed, and there's somebody either coming or going!'

Adam was naming all the animals. 'And that', he said to Eve, 'is a rhinoceros'.
  'Why call it a rhinoceros?' asked Eve.
  'Because,' said the First Man scornfully, 'it looks like a rhinoceros, stupid!'

'My wife's an angel.'
'Really? Mine's still alive.'

A priest was appalled to find a small boy sitting at the back of the church playing a pop tune on his mouth-organ. 'That's quite enough of that!' said the priest sternly. 'Don' you know the First Commandment?'

'No, Father,' replied the shaver, 'but you hum it and I'l try to follow you!'

Sunday School teacher: 'Hands up all those who want to go to Heaven? . . . Hands up . . . what about you, Terry? You haven't got your hand up — don't you want to go to Heaven?'
Terry: 'I can't. Me Mum told me to go straight home!'

Everyone in the Primary School was very excited over the forthcoming visit of the bishop. 'Now I want you all on your best behaviour,' said the headmaster, 'and if the bishop should address any of you children, you must speak up and call him My Lord.'

The great day arrived and the saintly bishop beamed upon the assembled tots. To one little boy he said kindly, 'And how old are you, my son?' Confused and over-awed the boy gasped out, 'Oh — er — My God, I'm six!'

A preacher was thrilled when a member of his congregation told him that his sermon had been like the peace and mercy of God. But the good preacher wasn't so pleased when he looked up the quotation in his Bible and found that it read: 'The peace of God passeth all understanding and his mercy endureth for ever'!

A certain preacher was extremely short in stature, but what he lacked in inches he more than made up for in fervour. One Sunday evening he climbed into his pulpit, the top of his head barely visible to the congregation. 'I am the Lamp of the Lord!' he declared. 'I am the Lamp of the Lord!'

At which a woman at the back of the church called out, 'Well, turn your wick up — we can't see you!'

An elderly pilgrim returning from Lourdes had arrived at Heathrow Airport, and on going through Customs said that he had nothing to declare. 'What's in this bottle?' asked the Customs officer.

'Oh, that's just holy water from the Lourdes spring,' said the pilgrim. But the Customs officer sniffed the contents, dipped in his finger, and licked it.

'This isn't holy water,' he said sternly, 'it's whisky!'

'St Bernadette be praised!' declared the pilgrim piously, 'another miracle!'

The Reverend Mr Smithers was a missionary, and was sent to a central African country. On arriving at his new post he sent a telegram to his wife in England. Unfortunately it was delivered by mistake to another Mrs Smithers whose husband had died only the day before. Just imagine her horror when she opened the telegram and read: ARRIVED SAFELY THIS MORNING. THE HEAT IS AWFUL!

Two astronauts knocked on the Pearly Gates, and St Peter answered. 'Come in, gentlemen,' said the Archangel. 'Just sit down there while I look up your files.'

'Oh, we don't want to come in,' said the first astronaut.

'You don't?' asked the astonished St Peter. 'What do you want then?'

'Please, sir,' said the second astronaut, 'can we have our capsule back?'

Arriving at a small village the travelling preacher asked a little boy for directions to the local church. The boy duly gave him directions, and the preacher said, 'Thank you, my son. I shall be giving a sermon in the church tonight and I'd like you and your Mummy and Daddy and all your friends to come.'

'What for?' asked the urchin suspiciously.

'Because,' explained the preacher, 'I want to tell you all how to find Heaven.'

'Don't make me laugh!' sneered the brat. 'You didn't even know where the church was!'

'Father! Father' said the young curate urgently to his parish priest. 'There's an old man in a long white beard sitting at the back of the church — he says he's God! What shall I do?'

'Go and keep an eye on him,' said the older priest, 'and try and look busy!'

The vicar's son was watching his father preparing the next Sunday's sermon.

'How do you know what to say, Daddy?' he asked.

'God tells me,' replied his reverend father.

'Then why do you keep crossing bits out?'

Little Susan was attending church for the very first time. 'What are all those people doing?' she asked her mother.

'Sssh, dear!' replied her mother. 'They're praying.'

'What — with all their clothes on?!'

'Was old Reverend Prendegast a successful missionary?'

'Certainly. He gave the tribesmen in Mbabaland their first taste of Christianity.'

Two ministers were talking, and one said, 'I had a terrible experience last Sunday. Absolutely awful!'

'What was that?' his brother minister asked in concern.

'Well, I dreamed that I was in my pulpit preaching,' said the first minister, 'and when I woke up — I found that I was!'

Two comedians were talking, and one said, 'I hear your agent got you a booking in the Vatican. Is that really true?'

'That's quite correct,' said the other, 'but I cancelled.'

'Cancelled?' exclaimed the first comedian. 'You cancelled a booking to entertain the Pope and all the Cardinals?'

'Well, how would you like to do *your* act in Latin?'

'And I'm afraid this is goodbye, God,' said the little girl as she finished her prayers. 'Tomorrow we're moving.'

Of course, Cain wanted to be as popular as his brother, but he turned nasty when he found out he wasn't Abel . . .

How does an airline pilot's child finish his prayers? 'God bless Mummy, God bless Daddy, and God bless me. Over and out.'

Young Esmeralda, a keen television viewer, was taken to her first church service. When asked by her Grannie how she had enjoyed it, she replied. 'The music and the singing were all right, but I didn't think much of the News.'

'Do you really believe Jonah was swallowed by a whale?'
  'When I get to Heaven I'll ask him.'
  'But suppose he's in the Other Place?'
  'Then you ask him.'

'It'd *better* rain,' muttered the kangaroo to his companion as they entered the Ark. 'We've hopped a long way for this.'

'Brother Damien, why is the chapel bell ringing this morning?'
  'Because Brother Augustine is pulling the rope, you silly fool!'

What does God have for his tea?
  Angel cakes.

What's the easiest way to get to Heaven quickly?
  Stand in the fast lane of a motorway.

A little boy went into the confessional box and said to the priest, 'Father, I threw peanuts into the river.' The priest couldn't see too much harm in that, so he gave the lad a light penance. Another boy entered the box and also said, 'Father, I threw peanuts into the river.' The priest was again puzzled, but not wishing to show his confusion sent the second boy away with a light penance. But in came another youngster—he'd thrown peanuts into the river as well—and the next boy, and the next! Then a very tiny mite came in, and the priest said, 'And I suppose you threw peanuts into the river?'
  'No, Father,' said the boy, 'I *am* Peanuts!'

'How did the wedding go today?' the churchwarden asked the verger.
  'Not too well, I'm afraid,' replied the verger. 'The vicar's squint got him into trouble again.'
  'Oh, no!' exclaimed the churchwarden. 'What did he do this time?'
  'He married the groom to the best man, kissed the register and locked the bride in the vestry safe!'

Little Amy was sent to church with two 10p pieces — one to put in the collection plate and the other to buy herself sweeties. But crossing the road the little girl tripped, and one of the coins dropped out of her hand, rolled along the pavement — and plopped down a grating!

'Sorry, Lord,' she said as she picked herself up. 'There goes your 10p!'

The Salvation Army girl was in the saloon bar with her collecting-tin, which she rattled under the nose of the oldest man in the bar. 'What's this for, then?' he growled.

'I'm collecting for the Lord,' she said.

'You'd better give me the tin, then,' he replied. 'I'll be seein' Him afore you, lass!'

The bishop was examining a confirmation class and wanted to make sure the children understood exactly what a bishop was. 'First of all,' he said, 'what am I?' There was a long silence; the children were puzzled by the question. 'Come along now,' repeated his lordship. 'What am I?'

And after a further pause a small voice said tentatively, 'You're a miserable sinner . . .'

In the pulpit was a passionate preacher; his voice rose in a great crescendo of triumph, then fell quavering in terror and pity. His arms flapped and flailed, his face glistened with fervour and the veins stood out upon his forehead, his eyes bulged and his nostrils quivered with righteousness. In the front pew was a small girl attending her first sermon. 'Mummy,' she whispered, having watched the fanatical preacher in growing alarm, 'what shall we do if he gets out?'

The airliner was forty thousand feet above the Atlantic when, to the passengers' horror, an announcement crackled from the cabin loudspeakers. 'This is your captain speaking! I regret to say we have an emergency. Two of our engines have failed. I have every expectation of reaching our destination safely but in the meantime will you please extinguish your cigarettes and fasten your safety-belts? Thank you.' One of the passengers, who was sitting next to a parson, immediately flew into a panic. 'Don't just sit there!' he screamed at his reverend neighbour. 'Do something religious!' So the parson took up a collection . . .

'I want to be good!' declared the penitent in the confessional. 'Can you help me, Father?'

'Of course I can, my son,' said the good priest comfortingly. 'The Lord is merciful.'

'Could you forgive someone who steals £30, Father?'

'Certainly, my son,' said the priest, 'but you must tell me all about this theft.'

'Well,' said the petty crook, 'there was £10 from Woolworth's yesterday and £10 from Tesco's today.'

'But that only makes £20.'

'Oh, I'll be getting the other £10 from Boots tomorrow!'

A Catholic priest and a Rabbi were discussing their respective financial arrangements. 'A third of the money we collect in the plate,' said the priest, 'goes to the Pope in Rome, a third goes to the bishop and the rest we can keep for ourselves.'

'I see, I see,' said the Rabbi. 'We do things a little differently. All the money we collect in the plate I put in a blanket; then my wife, my sons and myself take a corner each. We pray and then we toss all the money high in the air. Whatever God wants for Himself he keeps and whatever falls back on the blanket *we* keep!'

An Anglican minister and a taxi-driver both died at the same time, but to his chagrin the minister discovered that the taxi-driver had been sent to Heaven while he was consigned to the other place. 'Why should this be?' the aggrieved clergyman complained to St Peter. 'After all, I must have prayed to the Lord far more than that taxi-driver.'

'That may well be so,' replied St Peter. 'However, each time you gave a service everyone fell asleep, but when that taxi-driver gave *his* service everyone prayed!'

In which Biblical story is tennis mentioned?
When Moses served in Pharaoh's court . . .

Sunday School teacher: Mavis, why should we pray for grace?
Mavis: Er, 'cos she's a very naughty little girl, Miss?

Thieves who broke into a church were terrified to hear, as they approached the vestry in search of gold plate, a deep voice saying, 'I'm going to eat your arms . . . then your legs . . . then your head . . . and then your body!' With a shriek they hurtled back out through the window whence they had entered, tumbled down the ladder and scurried off as fast as their legs would carry them. Meanwhile, back at the vestry, the vicar was finishing the last of his favourite jelly-babies . . . 'I'm going to eat your arms . . .'

Did you hear about the little boy who was christened Glug-Glug?
The vicar dropped him in the font.

School Reports

Why are teachers special?
  'Cos they're in a class of their own.

What happens to the girl who misses the school bus?
  She catches it when she gets home.

'Anna, who was the first woman?'
  'Don't know, Miss.'
  'Come along, come along. It was something to do with an apple . . .'
  'Oh, yes, Miss. Granny Smith!'

'What did Sir think of your homework?'
  'He took it like a lamb.'
  'Really? What did he say?'
  'Baa!'

Tommy was late for school yet again, this time coming out with a spectacularly lurid and transparently false excuse.
  'Now then, Tommy,' said his teacher, 'do you know what happens to children who tell lies?'
  'Yes, Miss' said the impertinent lad. 'They become teachers!'

This year's class outing will be to the seaside!	Hooray!
It will cost £40 . . .	Boo!
. . . by train or £1.50 on the coach!	Hooray!
The headmaster will be coming . . .	Boo!
. . . to see us off!	Hooray!
The weather will be wet and windy . . .	Boo!
. . .in Russia and warm and sunny in Britain!	Hooray!
There will be no swimming . . .	Boo!
. . .until we get there!	Hooray!
Lunch will be boiled fish and cabbage . . .	Boo!
. . . for me and crisps and Coke and Smarties for you!	Hooray!
There will be a visit to the museum . . .	Boo!
. . . or if preferred to the Funfair!	Hooray!
But we must be back by twelve o'clock . . .	Boo!
. . . at midnight!	Hooray!

'Sarah,' said the teacher, 'what is a cannibal?'
  'Dunno, Miss.'
  'Well, if you were to eat your parents, what would you be?'
  'An orphan, Miss.'

'Mum, I don't wanna go to school! I don't wanna go to school!'

'Now, dear, you must go, and for two very good reasons. First, you're fifty-six years of age and second you're the Headmaster!'

'William, why are you late for school again?'

'Sorry, Miss, but I dreamed I was playing football and the game went into extra time!'

'Viola, can you spell "banana" for me?'

'Well, Sir, I know how to start but I don't know when to stop.'

'How old would you say I am, Francis?' the teacher asked.

'Forty, Sir,' said the boy promptly.

'You seem very sure,' said the puzzled teacher. 'What makes you think I am forty?'

'My big brother's twenty, Sir,' replied the boy 'and you're twice as daft as he is!'

'Melanie!' said the teacher sharply, 'you've been doing Rebecca's homework for her again! I recognized your handwriting in her exercisebook.'

'No, I haven't, Miss, declared Melanie. 'It's just that we both use the same pencil!'

'Jarvis — I hope I didn't see you copying just then : . .?'

'I hope you didn't as well!'

'Philip,' asked the chemistry mistress, 'what is HNO_3?'

'Oh, er . . . just a minute, Miss . . . er . . . it's on the tip of my tongue, Miss . . .'

'Well in that case — spit it out. It's nitric acid!'

'Theo, why were you absent from school yesterday?'

'Oh, er, I wasn't well, Miss. Had a bit of a temperature.'

'I see. And do you have a note from your Mother or your Father?'

'No, Miss.'

'I shall expect to see one tomorrow. Is that clear?'

'Yes. Miss.'

Next day Theo handed in the following note: 'Dear Miss, Theo was absent from skool on Toosday on account of a cold. Yours faithfully, My Father.'

'Selena, why are you late this time?'

'Sorry, Sir, but I was in good time walking along the High Street until I saw a road sign that said Go Slow. So I did!'

What must you pay when you go to school?

Attention.

The headmaster was amazed at the improvement in work and behaviour of his school's most notoriously unruly form — all the more so since a new teacher had taken over only that term. 'Well done, Miss Blenkinsop!' he said warmly. 'But tell me, how do you keep your class on their toes?'

'Put drawing-pins on their seats!'

A girl was sent home by an angry teacher for not attending in school uniform. She returned half an hour later dripping wet. 'What's the meaning of this?' demanded her teacher. 'You told me to wear my school clothes,' said the miserable pupil, 'but they were in the wash!'

'Sir!' said Alexander. 'Empty Coke tins, fish-and-chip paper, plastic bag, used tissues, broken bottles, empty cardboard boxes — '

'Alexander!' snapped the teacher. 'You're talking rubbish again!'

'Now Frank,' said the weary maths master, 'if you had £7 in one pocket and £7 in another pocket, what would you have?'

'Someone else's trousers on!'

'Miss! Miss! cried little Jamie, 'I just banged my fumb on the door!'

'Not "fumb", Jamie,' said the teacher. 'It's *th*umb!'

'Yes, Miss. And I banged my thinger as well!'

'Sir, you know you told us yesterday that a pound of feathers was the same as a pound of lead?'

'Yes. what about it?'

'My Dad said you were wrong. He said I should try tickling your toes with a pound of lead!'

'Our new P.E. master thinks that exercise is so good for you it'll solve all your problems.'

'I know. Doesn't matter what's wrong he reckons that gym'll fix it!'

I won't say our school-dinners are bad but even the dustbins have ulcers!

'Why are you home from school so early, Jackie?'

'I was sent home, Mum, 'cos the boy next to me was smoking.'

'But if *he* was smoking why should *you* be sent home?'

'It was me that set him alight!'

A young shaver called Jimmy Mickey Rigsby was complaining to his mother about his new teacher. 'My name is Jimmy Mickey Rigsby, isn't it, Mum?' 'Yes, of course,' replied his mother soothingly. 'Why do you ask?' 'Well, my teacher says it's too long and just calls me Jimmy Rigsby.' 'What's wrong with that?' 'I don't like having the Mickey taken out of me!'

P.E. Teacher: 'Alison, you're hopeless at sports. You'll never come first in anything.'
Alison: 'I'm first every day in the dinner queue, Miss!'

The primary class had been told to draw a scene representing the flight into Egypt. One little tot proudly displayed a drawing of a Jumbo Jet containing the three members of the Holy Family — but also a fourth figure. 'When I said "flight" I didn't quite mean a jet-plane,' said the teacher. 'However, we'll let that pass for now. But who is the fourth person on the plane?' To which the little one replied, 'That's Pontius Pilot!'

Andy came home from his first day at school weeping buckets. 'What's the matter, Andy?' asked his worried parents. 'It's the school dinner,' he sobbed. 'It was awful! I couldn't touch it, and I'm hungry!' 'I'm sure it can't have been that bad,' said his father. 'What was the dinner?' 'Worms and cow-muck!' came the astounding reply. Andy's mother immediately telephoned the school and spoke to the Headmistress. 'Andy's very upset about today's school meal,' she said. 'Can you tell me what it was?' 'Certainly,' said the Head. 'Spaghetti bolognaise!'

Paul was on the carpet in the Headmaster's office. 'Your form teacher has been complaining to me about you,' said the Head sternly. 'What have you been doing?'
    'Nothing, Sir,' said Paul miserably, to which the Head replied, 'Precisely!'

'Philip, what does it mean when the barometer falls?'
    'Er — the nail's come out of the wall, Miss?'

Geography Teacher: 'Monica, where are the Andes?'
Monica: 'At the end of your armies, Sir!'

Stewart owned a very small newt of which he was extremely fond, so much so that he couldn't bear to be parted from it even when going to school. One day his teacher spotted him at his desk gazing intently into a matchbox. 'What have you got there, Stewart?' demanded the teacher. 'It's a newt, Miss' replied the boy. 'Why do you keep it in a matchbox?' asked the teacher, to which Stewart replied, 'Because it's my newt!' (Minute)

At a school concert one of the teachers noticed that little Dorothy seemed unable to clap her hands — whenever she tried they kept missing each other. After the concert the teacher took Dorothy aside and tried to teach her how to clap properly, but without success. 'You try and practise over the weekend,' said the kindly teacher, 'and if you can clap properly on Monday I'll buy you an ice-cream.'
    So all over the weekend little Dorothy practised hard, and on the Monday she triumphantly displayed to the teacher her new-found powers of co-ordination.
    'Well done, Dorothy,' said the teacher. 'Come into the playground at break and I'll buy you an ice-cream from the

Mr Whippy van at the school gate.' And true to his promise at break the teacher bought Dorothy a huge cornet which he handed to the little girl, who took it delightedly and went — *(bring up your closed fist and bang it on your forehead)* slap!

In the changing room after a football match the P.E. master asked whether any of the boys had seen his glasses. 'I saw them on the pitch, Sir,' answered Harry.

'Well, why didn't you bring them in?' asked the teacher.

'I thought you didn't want them any more, Sir,' said Harry, 'so I stepped on them!'

'Gary, did your sister help you with this homework?'

'No, Miss. She did it all!'

History teacher: 'Georgina, in the second World War the Germans conquered Poland, they conquered France, they conquered Belgium, Holland, Denmark and several other countries. But why didn't they conquer Britain?

Georgina: 'Er — 'cos they'd run out of conkers, Sir?'

Shaggy Dog Stories

And Other Tall Tails

Brother Benedict had been a monk for many, many years, and was delighted to be told by his Superior one day that he had a visitor. He rushed to the parlour and found that the caller was none other than an old friend from his schooldays. They were reminiscing happily when, deep in the cellars of the monastery, came a tremendous crash and a long, mournful howl. 'What on earth was that?' asked the visitor, startled. 'I'm sorry, Andrew,' said Brother Benedict, 'but I am bound to secrecy by my Holy Vows, and as you are not a monk I cannot tell you.'

After another half an hour Andrew left, still puzzled by the subterranean mystery, and promising to visit his old friend should he ever happen to be in the vicinity again. But it was to be ten long years before he returned; ten long years before he was sitting again in the monastery parlour with Brother Benedict. 'Now you can tell me what is going on in the cellars here,' said Andrew, 'for as you can see from my habit I have become a monk myself, and for ten long years I have wondered what caused that crash and that howl.'

At this point you say 'And do you know what caused the crash and the howl in the cellar . . . No? . . . Well, I can't tell you because you're not a monk!'

Conrad lived in a four-bedroomed house. He went into the first bedroom where his father was busy decorating, and said, 'Dad, I think you're putting that wallpaper up the wrong way.' To which his father replied, 'Who's decorating this room — you or me?' So Conrad went into the second bedroom of his four-bedroomed house where his brother was making a model aircraft. 'Oliver,' he said, 'I think you're putting that wing on wrongly.' To which his brother replied, 'Who's making this aircraft — you or me?' So Conrad went into the fourth bedroom of his four-bedroomed house —

At which point you will be asked 'But what about the third bedroom?' To which you reply, 'Who's telling this story — you or me?'

There was once a fabulously wealthy man who lived far from civilization in a huge Golden House. Everything about the house was Golden — the bricks, the doors, the floors, the furniture, the knives and forks; everything that could possibly be Golden was indeed of pure, finest quality Gold. One night, as the fabulously wealthy man lay in his Golden Bed between his Golden Sheets, there came a ring on the Golden Bell. He rose, put on his Golden Dressing-Gown, walked down the Golden Passage to the Golden Stairs and thence down to the Golden Hall where he opened the Golden Door. 'I'm sorry to bother you,' said the stranger on the Golden Doorstep, 'but my car has broken down and this seems to be the only house for miles and miles. Could you possibly put me up for the night?' 'Of course,' said the fabulously wealthy man, 'follow me'. And he took the stranger through the Golden Hall, up the Golden Stairs and along the Golden Passage. 'You may sleep here,' he said, 'in this Golden Bedroom. In the Golden Cupboard you will find a pair of Golden Pyjamas. Sleep well.'

The fabulously wealthy man returned to his Golden Bed and was just falling into a light doze when again the Golden Bell roused him. It was a second stranger whose car had broken down, and he was also shown to a Golden Bedroom. Similarly a third stranded stranger who rang the Golden Bell a half hour or so later was lodged in yet another Golden Bedroom.

In the morning the three travellers found themselves in a huge Golden Breakfast room. They sat at a vast Golden Table as a servant entered, wearing Golden livery and a powdered Golden Wig. 'What would you like for breakfast, gentlemen?' he asked. 'Cornflakes or kippers?'

'I'll have cornflakes,' said the first.

'I'll have cornflakes as well,' said the second.

'I'll have kippers, please,' said the third.

Which proves that two out of three people prefer cornflakes for breakfast . . .

(As you begin this story you say to your listener, 'You're the bus driver, right? Don't forget.')

A bus carrying four passengers stopped at the first stop and five people got on; at the next stop six got off and ten got on; at the next stop one got on but nobody got off. At the next stop nobody got on but three got off; at the next stop the bus went straight past, to the consternation of an old lady who hadn't realized it was a request stop. However, at the next stop she did get off, and a couple got on. There was one more stop to go before the bus reached the terminus; only one got on here, and at the terminus of course everybody got off. Now, what was the bus driver's name?

(By this time your listener will have completely forgotten the beginning of the story and will invariably say, 'I don't know'. To which you reply, 'Yours — you're the driver, remember!?')

Checking his football coupon one Saturday evening Mr Spendmore realized to his joy that he had won a first dividend prize! On the Monday he rushed down to his place of work and resigned; then he wrote out cheques for a Rolls-Royce, ten suits, an ocean-going yacht, a mansion in the country, and a huge diamond ring. All that week he threw parties and gave presents to all his friends and relatives. But the following Monday saw Mr Spendmore back at his office, asking for his job back. 'Fed up with being one of the idle rich, Spendmore?' asked his boss. 'Is that what last week has taught you?'

'Not exactly,' said Mr Spendmore. 'It's taught me never to trust my wife to post my coupon for me!'

On his eighteenth birthday Jeremy was given a superb Victorian pocket-watch by his father. 'Take great care of it,' said his father. 'That's a family heirloom — my great-grandfather gave it to my grandfather, my grandfather gave it to my father, and now I am giving it to you. Good luck, my boy, and I hope I live long enough to see you hand it on to your son.'

A few weeks later Jeremy was watching a variety show. The last act before the interval was a magician, who asked for the loan of a watch. So up went Jeremy on to the stage where he handed over the precious gift. 'Thank you,' said the magician. 'Now, watch carefully as I place this beautiful timepiece in this envelope . . . I seal it down . . . thank you.'

The magician then produced a large hammer, placed the envelope on a table, and smashed the hammer down upon it with all his might! He pounded and pounded — and then paused: something had obviously gone awry, for small wheels and cogs and springs and bits of metal were flying around in all directions — the watch was smashed to smithereens! Utterly beyond repair! Jeremy rushed off the stage, ran up the centre aisle to the manager's office and burst in furiously.

'That fool has smashed up my lovely watch!' he roared.

'Calm yourself, sir, please!' said the manager smoothly. 'Do sit down. Would you care for a cup of tea?'

But Jeremy was not so easily fobbed off. 'Now look here, what about my — ?'

'Do you take milk?' asked the manager.

'Oh, er, yes. Just a splash. But what about —'

'Sugar?'

'Two lumps please. But what about — ?'

'Here you are, sir,' said the manager with a smile as he handed Jeremy the cup of tea. And what do you think he handed Jeremy with the cup?

(Your listener is bound to say 'The watch'. To which you reply, 'No — a chocky bicky!')

The Chicago Kid loved to gamble for very high stakes. Unfortunately the Chicago kid was also very unlucky, eventually losing his car, his house, his business, his family, his friends — everything. In his wretchedness he entered a church and fell to his kness.

'Just give me a big win tonight, Guardian Angel,' he implored with tears running down his face, 'and I swear I'll never gamble again.' And to his astonishment he heard a small voice in his ear which said, 'Very well, Kid. If you are sincere I'll help you. Just this once.'

Overjoyed, the Kid rushed off to the casino where he stood at the roulette wheel, his last ten dollars in his trembling hand, waiting for guidance. 'Put the ten dollars on Red Number Twelve!' said that small clear voice in his ear. Ashen-faced, the Kid did as his Guardian Angel instructed. The wheel was spun, the ball was thrown; it skipped and danced round the wheel and finally came to rest — in Red Number Twelve! The Kid had won! As he reached forward to pick up his winnings he heard again that small, clear voice. 'Leave it there, Kid. Let it ride!' And the Kid obediently withdrew his hand, leaving his winnings still on Red Number Twelve.

With sweat running down his face and his knees knocking, the Chicago Kid watched the little silver ball again skipping and dancing round the spinning wheel. 'In seconds,' he thought, 'all my worries will be over! I'll be rich!' And the little silver ball dropped neatly into — Red Number Thirteen! As the Chicago Kid, numb with horror, gazed incredulously at the now still wheel, the small, clear voice in his ear said, *'Blast . . . !'*

One wild and stormy winter's evening a young girl called Sandra was called by her mother. 'Daddy and I have to go out for a couple of hours,' she said. 'Will you be all right on your own?'

'Of course I will, Mummy,' said the self-possessed young lady, but after her parents had left, a sudden loud noise made her jump — but then she laughed to herself. It was only the telephone! However, when Sandra lifted the receiver, all she could hear was a gasping, eerie voice which said, 'My name is Bloody-Fingers! I am coming to your house! I'll be there in five minutes!'

With a terrified sob Sandra slammed the receiver down and ran up to the attic; she locked the door behind her, pushed a heavy trunk against it and then crawled into the farthest, darkest corner of the attic and lay, shaking with fright, under an old carpet.

Scarcely had she reached this hiding-place when the sound of crashing, splintering wood above the howling of the wind told the frightened girl that the front door had been broken open; she heard heavy, dragging footsteps coming along the hall and up the stairs. And then, to her unspeakable horror, the attic door was also forced open and the heavy trunk pushed aside! Peeping out from under the carpet, she saw dimly, by flashes of lightning, a huge, hideous, wild-eyed, shaggy-haired man lurching towards her. As he drew closer she saw — oh, horrible! — that both his hand were dripping with blood! 'What do you want?!' she screamed.

And again she heard that awful, sepulchral voice. 'I am Bloody-Fingers!' said the vile creature stretching out his hands towards her, 'and please — could I have some Elastoplast?'

After spending the evening in the local pub a man emerged at closing time to find a storm raging. The wind was howling and the rain was lashing down, so he decided to take a short cut through the churchyard. It was very dark and spooky walking between the gravestones with the thunder booming and the lightning crackling, but the man pressed on — until, above the noise of the storm, he thought he heard a tapping sound. His curiosity getting the better of his nervousness he followed the sound until suddenly, by the glare of prolonged flashes of lightning, he saw this weird old man, dressed in what appeared to be a white sheet, tapping away at a headstone with a hammer and chisel. 'What are you doing?' asked the man, his surprise mingled with terror.

'I'm putting this headstone right,' said the creature. 'They've spelt my name wrong . . .!'

A squid was swimming through the ocean when he met his friend Mr Whale. 'And how are you today, Mr Squid?' asked Mr Whale. 'Oh, I'm not too well at all,' said Mr Squid gloomily. 'I don't know what's the matter with me.'

'Oh dear,' said Mr Whale sympathetically. 'Why don't you take my advice? Whenever I'm feeling out of sorts I always swim a little deeper. If I were you I'd go down fifty feet; I'm sure you'll feel better then.'

'I don't think I can swim any deeper,' replied Mr Squid. 'I'm not heavy enough.'

'Well, let me help you,' said the obliging Mr Whale, and he pushed Mr Squid down and down and down, when suddenly there appeared from behind a rock Mr Squid's arch-enemy, Mr Shark!

'Hello, Mr Shark,' said Mr Whale cheerily. 'Here's that sick squid I owe you!'

One Saturday night a latecomer sidled into the Army camp a full fifteen minutes after his pass had expired. The orderly sergeant asked for an explanation, and the defaulter replied, 'I tried to get a taxi, Sarge, but they was all busy. So I spotted this bloke with a horse and cart and offered him a quid to give me a lift. But half-way up the hill the horse dropped dead, so I had to walk the rest of the way.'

'Do you think I'm going to fall for a ridiculous story like that?' roared the orderly sergeant. 'You're on a charge! Lock him in the guardhouse!'

Just then another latecomer arrived at the camp gate. 'And where do you think you've been?' demanded the sergeant ominously. 'Well, Sarge, it was like this,' explained the second defaulter. 'I couldn't find a taxi anywhere, but I spotted this geezer with a horse and cart and I offered him a quid for a lift. But half-way up the hill the horse dropped dead so I had to walk.'

'You idle layabout!' yelled the orderly sergeant. 'I've never heard such a cock-and-bull story! You're on a charge! Lock him up!' And as the cell door clanged shut behind the second latecomer a third arrived puffing out apologies.

'And I suppose you couldn't find a taxi, eh?' asked the sergeant heavily, tapping his highly-polished toe. 'Oh, I got a taxi all right,' came the reply.

'You did? Then why are you so late?'

'Couldn't get up the hill for dead horses.'

Once upon a time were three little worms called Foot, Foot-Foot, and Foot-Foot-Foot. One day, as they were crossing the road to do their shopping, Foot was run over by a steam-roller and squashed flat. Terrible tragedy! Of course Foot-Foot and Foot-Foot-Foot were extremely upset, but a day or two after the funeral Foot-Foot said to Foot-Foot-Foot, 'I know we've had an awful shock, but life goes on and we must still do the shopping.'

'Yes, I suppose you're right,'' sighed Foot-Foot-Foot to Foot-Foot. 'But we must be very careful. After all, we've got one Foot in the grave already!'

A traveller stranded miles from anywhere decided to spend the night in an old, rather creepy inn. 'We have one room vacant,' said the landlord, 'which we don't usually let out. There is a trapdoor in the centre of the room and I must ask you not, on any account, to open it. Do you understand? *Do not open the trapdoor!'*

Naturally the traveller agreed and was shown into the room, which seemed very cosy and comfortable — except for the trapdoor. He could not take his eyes off it, wondering what secret lay hidden beneath. His curiosity finally got the better of him; he grasped the ring set into its centre and slowly pulled. The trapdoor rose protestingly, and a musty smell assailed the traveller's nostrils as he peered into the blackness below. What was that? Something seemed to be moving . . . he put out a hand — and touched a hideous, icy-cold, jelly-like *Thing*! With the shriek of a soul tormented he ran out of the room, down the stairs and out into the night with the vile, nightmarish *Thing* pursuing him.

He ran and ran until he reached a lake where, providentially, he found a rowing-boat: surely that ghastly clammy creature would not be able to follow him across water? But it could, and it did! The traveller rowed and rowed till he thought his heart would crack, the fearful blob floating in his wake. In the centre of the lake he spied an island; gasping, exhausted he threw himself ashore and curled up in an agony of terror to wait his fate.

The *Thing* emerged from the water and slid towards him until its rank odoriferous presence all but engulfed him. He shuddered as a foul tentacle extruded itself from the seething mass, and a ghoulish voice whispered sibilantly, 'You're *It*!'

The girl walked into the dark, dark house through the dark, dark hall and down the dark, dark stairs to the dark, dark cellar where there was a dark, dark passageway at the end of which was a dark, dark room. Inside was a dark, dark cupboard and inside that was an electrician mending the fuse.

Two wicked men decided to dig up the grave of a woman who had been buried with a valuable ring on her finger. But try as they might they were unable to pull the ring off the corpse's hand. 'We'll have to cut the finger off!' said one of the robbers.

'All right,' said the other evil villain. 'I'll do it!'

With the ring in their possession the sinister pair made off into the night. Whereupon a great storm blew up and they began to look around for shelter. In the distance they saw a light, and on approaching saw that it came from a gloomy and strangely forbidding old house. 'Let's ask if we can stay the night here,' said one of the robbers. So they knocked on the door, and a hideous old crone bid them enter. 'Would you gentlemen care for some supper?' she asked, cackling weirdly. 'Oh, yes please!' they answered, and the old woman took them to the kitchen where she instructed them to sit at a bare wooden table. As she served the food to the hungry pair they noticed that she had a finger missing from her hand! In trembling tones one of the robbers said, 'What happened to your finger?'

And the old crone fixed him with a terrible gaze and said, 'YOU'VE GOT IT!'

(This story should be told very quietly, and then the last three words yelled out!)

'Sir, what's a gumblestrode?' asked the schoolboy innocently.

'How dare you!' roared the angry teacher. 'Go to the headmaster at once!'

In the headmaster's office the puzzled schoolboy repeated his question. 'You wretched boy!' yelled the headmaster. 'Get out! And don't come back!'

Home trudged the unhappy and bewildered lad. 'You're back early,' said his father. 'What's up?'

'The headmaster told me to get out,' said the boy, ''cos I asked what a gumblestrode was.'

'What?' snapped his father. 'Get out! Get out of this house! And don't come back!'

In tears the boy wandered the streets until he was spotted by a policeman on his beat. 'You're out very late, young man,' said the officer. 'Have you no home to go to?' 'No,' snuffled the miserable youngster. 'And all because I asked what a gumblestrode was.'

'Did you, indeed?' snapped the policeman. 'This is a very serious matter. You'd better come with me to the station!' This was too much for the boy; he evaded the policeman's grasp and ran and ran as fast as he could. 'Stop that boy!' shouted the officer as he chased in hot pursuit, but as his quarry ran across a main road a lorry knocked him down and killed him . . .

A man staying alone one night in a reputedly haunted house was alarmed to be woken by a mysterious rapping sound. It seemed to be coming from somewhere downstairs, so he got up, put on his dressing-gown and cautiously went down to the hall. Still he could hear the rapping noise — was it coming from the cellar? Down the cellar steps he went, and the rapping sounded louder and louder. In the cellar was a large cupboard — the rapping was definitely emanating from there! Trembling with fear but determined to discover the cause of the sound, the man opened the cupboard door …and inside was a large box. Yes, the box was definitely the source of the rapping! Shaking with terror he opened the box — and discovered a sheet of wrapping paper . . .

An Englishman, an Irishman and a Scotsman were in goal, and were sentenced to be whipped. 'Before I start,' said the man with the whip, 'I must inform you that by prison rules you are each permitted to have something on your backs to ease the pain.' He then said to the Irishman, 'What will you have?' 'I'll have some Irish whisky on my back,' said the Irishman who had heard that spirit was good for cuts and bruises. So Irish whisky was rubbed on the Irishman's back and he was duly whipped. 'And what will you have on your back?' the Scotsman was asked; 'Scotch whisky!' he declared stoutly. And Scotch whisky was rubbed on his back and he was whipped. Then came the Englishman's turn. 'And what will you have on your back?' he was asked, to which he replied, 'The Irishman!'

An Englishman, an Irishman and a Scotsman were sentenced to live in a deep pit for ten years, but they were allowed one request each. 'I'll have ten years' supply of Scotch whisky!' said the Scotsman. 'I'll have ten years' supply of Irish whisky!' said the Irishman. 'I'll have ten years' supply of cigarettes!' said the Englishman. After ten years they were released; the Scotsman staggered out of the pit and immediately fell dead from alcoholic poisoning. The Irishman also climbed out and fell dead from alcoholic poisoning, but the Englishman climbed out and said 'Anybody got a light?'

Two astronauts called Jan Hans and Alfred Knees landed on an unexplored planet, where they found a peculiar unknown species of flower. The strange thing about this flower was that it kept emitting an eerie booming sound, and so Jan Hans and Alfred Knees decided to take a specimen back to earth for detailed botanical examination. Back home it was decided that, as this strange flower looked something like a daisy, it should be christened Hans-Knees-and-Booms-a-Daisy . . .

'See this ball-point pen, Brendan? It's the finest in the world. Cost a fortune, but worth every penny. It will write in the hottest deserts, in the Arctic wastes, underwater, in outer space — anywhere and in any environment, it will function exactly the same.'

'I've got one like that,' replied Brendan not a whit abashed. 'Cost me 20p at Woollies. Functions exactly the same wherever you take it.'

'For 20p? How's that?'

'It doesn't work.'

A farmer's wife prepared a huge vat of dye in her kitchen garden in order to dye her curtains. Unfortunately one of the lambs wandered into the kitchen garden and fell into the vat. It struggled out a bright pink colour, and try as she might the farmer's wife was unable to get the lamb back to its original fleecy white. But as luck would have it a sheep breeder spotted this pink lamb in the field and, deciding it was a new and potentially rare type, offered ten times the normal price to buy it. The farmer's wife shrewdly promised the breeder more pink lambs, and duly dyed as many lambs as were required to make her and her husband's fortune. So that today she is the biggest lamb dyer in the country . . .

An Englishman, an Irishman and an American were standing at the edge of a fifty foot cliff. 'I'll give $1,000 to whichever of you guys has got the courage to jump over the edge,' said the American. Naturally the Englisman and the Irishman refused. 'Let's see you do it,' they said — and the American immediately leapt off the cliff, landing lightly and unharmed on his toes! So the Englishman jumped off — only to land *splat* on the rocks below; the Irishman jumped off — and he landed *splat* on the rocks. The American then went home and told his wife what had happened. 'Oh, that was very naughty of you,' she declared. 'Why didn't you tell them you were Superman!'

Three months before his birthday, little Godfrey was asked by his mother what he would like. 'A ping-pong ball, Mum!' came the immediate answer. A puzzled mother discussed this strange request with Godfrey's father, who also asked the boy what he would like for his birthday. 'A ping-pong ball, Dad!' again was the answer. Every few weeks the question was repeated, and the same answer — 'A ping-pong ball!' — was always given. Finally Godfrey's birthday arrived, and the small package was handed over. The elated Godfrey rushed up to his bedroom tearing the wrapping-paper off his long-awaited present. Mystified, his parents tiptoed up the stairs and peeped in through the door. 'Oh,' said Godfrey's father, 'so *that's* what you wanted a ping-pong ball for . . .!'

Dan Dare was taken prisoner on an alien planet and was about to be executed. 'You can't do that to me!' protested the great space explorer. 'I'm a very important person back on Earth. If you execute me it will mean a lot of trouble for you!'

'So you're a big wheel back on Earth, are you?' sneered the alien leader. 'Well, if you're so famous I suppose everyone on your world will know you?'

'Certainly,' replied Dan Dare, 'everyone knows me!'

'Very well,' said the alien leader, 'let us prepare a little test. We will take you secretly back to Earth, and if the first Earthling we come across does not know you, you will instantly be put to death!'

So off went the alien spaceship to Earth, with Dan Dare and his captors aboard. As chance would have it they landed by a cottage in a remote part of Ireland; the alien leader, with Dan Dare being dragged along behind him in chains, marched up to the door and banged sharply. And from upstairs they heard an old lady call out, 'Who dat Dan Dere?'

An Englishman, an Irishman and a Scotsman were hiding from bandits up palm trees. The bandit chief called up one tree, 'Who's there?' And the Englishman went 'Cheep! Cheep!' like a bird. So the bandit chief called up the next tree, 'Who's there?' And the Scotsman went 'Eeek! Eeek!' like a monkey. So the bandit chief called up the next tree, 'Who's there?' And the Irishman went, 'Moo-oo!'

An Englishman, an Irishman and a nun were playing darts. The Englishman threw first and the master of ceremonies called out 'One hundred and twenty!' The nun threw next and the master of ceremonies called out 'One hundred and sixty!' Then the Irishman threw — but the poor nun had not had a chance to get out of the way, so the master of ceremonies called out, 'One nun dead and eighty!'

A naturalist spent six months in the darkest South American jungle hunting for an extremely rare caterpillar. Finally he found one marvellous specimen, which he placed carefully in a special container. The container was placed in a packing-case, and the packing-case was placed in a lead box — to make quite sure that the caterpillar reached the London Zoo safely. But when the naturalist opened the lead box, the packing-case and then the special container — no caterpillar was to be seen! Despondent at the thought of six months' work wasted, the naturalist decided to make himself a cup of tea. He turned on the tap to fill the kettle — and what do you think came out? *(You will of course receive the answer 'the caterpillar', to which you reply)* No, water!

A terrible thing happened to me yesterday! I was with my Mum in the supermarket doing some shopping. She asked me to look after her basket while she went to get something from the other end of the store, and while I was waiting the manager came up and said I was trying to steal! He took me into his office and said he was going to ring for the police; I was so scared, and I knew my Mum would be wondering where I had got to, so I leaned out of the window to see if I could see her. Well, the manager thought I was trying to escape, so he pulled my leg . . . just as I'm pulling yours now!

A traveller stuck miles from anywhere in the country was relieved to find a small hotel; the bad news was that it looked extremely uninviting and sinister. However, the traveller didn't fancy spending the night in his car, and so he found himself applying for a room. All seemed quite normal, if somewhat quiet, and the only thing he found disturbing was a large red push-button by the door of his room. What was it for? There was no notice to explain its function, so what could it be? An alarm bell? A service bell? All night long he lay, tossing and turning, worrying about the purpose of the mysterious button. By morning he was absolutely exhausted, not having had so much as a second's sleep. He wearily packed his bag, but just as he was leaving to go downstairs for breakfast, his curiosity got the better of him. Plucking up his courage he jabbed firmly at the red button — and the centre light came on . . .

Three knights were arguing as to which of them was the bravest. 'I fought a dragon in the air,' said the first, 'and cut its head off!' 'I fought a dragon under the sea,' said the second, 'and cut its tail off!' 'I cut the tail off a snail,' said the third. 'That's not very brave!' scoffed the other two. 'Well,' came the reply, 'it was a dragon (dragging) on the ground!'

An Englishman, an Irishman and a Scotsman had gone mountaineering. An avalanche had cut off the way forward and the way back, leaving them stuck on the very edge of a precipitous drop of two thousand metres. While they were debating between themselves what was to be done a fairy appeared. 'I can see your predicament,' said the fairy, 'and I will help you if I can. You may have one wish each, but my powers are limited and I can only change you into birds.'
'Very well,' said the Englishman, 'I'll be an eagle.' The fairy waved her magic wand, and immediately the Englishman was changed into a noble eagle; he stepped off the edge of the precipice and soared away to safety.
'I'll be a hawk,' said the Scotsman — again the fairy waved her wand and the Scotsman, now a beautiful hawk, soared away to safety.
'What bird would you like to be?' said the fairy to the Irishman. 'Er, a penguin' said the Irishman . . .

Another Englishman, another Irishman and another Scotsman were also trapped on a cliff edge, when again the Good Fairy appeared. 'I can help you out of your predicament, gentlemen,' she declared. 'I can grant you one wish each — you can choose wherever you would like to be.'
The Englishman immediately stepped foward. 'England,' he said — and straightaway the Good Fairy magicked him back to England.
The Scotsman stepped forward. 'Scotland!' he declared — and straightaway he found himself back in Scotland.
The Irishman stepped forward and stumbled over a rock, 'Oh hell . . .!' he muttered — and straightaway . . . .

Situations Vacant

or Mind Your Own Business

'My brother's got a good job.'
  'What's that?'
  'Test pilot for Kleenex.'

Who earns a living by driving customers away?
  A taxi-driver.

'I'm the boss and you're nothing! What are you?'
  'Nothing.'
  'And what am I?'
  'Boss over nothing.'
  'Pshaw! You're next to an idiot.'
  'Very well. I'll move.'

'My grandfather was a ship's carpenter. He was a champion poopdeck maker. He made five hundred poopdecks and then he died.'
  'Why?'
  'He was all pooped out.'

'Are you still working in that florist's?'
  'No, I got the sack.'
  'Why?'
  'I had to put the cards into the floral tributes and I got two of them mixed up. The flowers going to a wedding I thought were going to a funeral, so I put in a card which read 'With Deepest Sympathy' . . . and the flowers going to the funeral had a wedding card in them.'
  'What did it say?'
  'Hope You'll Be Happy In Your New Home!'

At a business conference a self-made millionaire approached the managing director of a rival company and said, 'I started my business life working for you.'
  'Really, Sir Henry?' said the managing director. 'I'm afraid I don't recall . . .'
  'Yes, indeed,' said the millionaire smugly. 'Thirty years ago I started as an office boy for your company. Do you remember giving me a message to deliver to the despatch department?'
  'Oh, yes, Sir Henry,' said the managing director. 'Now I remember. Any reply?'

'Boss, there's a man here to see you.'
   'Tell him to take a chair.'
   'Why, is he buying old furniture?'

'Is it difficult to be a coroner?'
   'Oh, yes. You have to take a stiff exam.'

'Why do you want to be an astronomer?'
   'I should think it's a heavenly job!'

'I want a hair-cut, please.'
   'Certainly, sir. Which one?'

'How's the trampoline-selling business?'
   'Oh, up and down.'

'Did you hear about old Harry? He's become a big-time operator.'
   'Really? What does he do?'
   'Winds up Big Ben.'

'This loaf is nice and warm!'
   'It should be — the cat's been sitting on it all day!'

'Mr Butcher, have you got a sheep's head?'
   'No, madam, it's just the way I part my hair.'

'Two pounds of cats' meat, please.'
   'Certainly, sir. Shall I wrap it or will you eat it here?'

'I say, waiter! Are you in the Union?'
   'Yes, sir. I'm the chop steward.'

What job has plenty of openings?
   A doorman.

Why did the lazy man get a job in a bakery?
   'Cos he wanted a good loaf.

'Late again, Slattery? Why don't you get an alarm clock?'
   'I did, sir, but it keeps going off while I'm asleep!'

'I say, waiter! Why is there a yellow line round my table?'
   'Oh, you'd better move, sir. There's no waiting there.'

'I say, waiter! There are five flies in my soup!'
   'Gosh, sir! Just one more and you'd have a world record!'

Did you hear about the worker in a banana-packing firm?
He got the sack for throwing the bent ones away . . .

A boy went into a pet-shop and said to the man behind the counter, 'Have you got any parrot-seed?'
'Oh, you've got a parrot, have you?' said the man.
'No,' said the boy, 'but I'd like to grow one!'

'What would you like?' asked the man in the chip shop.
'Shark and chips,' replied the customer. 'And make it snappy!'

A diner in a restaurant was handed the menu by the waiter who, the diner was disconcerted to observe, stood by the table scratching his bottom. 'I say, waiter,' said the customer icily, 'have you got an itchy bottom?'
'No, sir,' replied the waiter. 'Only what's on the menu!'

'I say, waiter! There's a fly in my soup!'
'Well, throw him a doughnut — they make super lifebelts!'

'I say, waiter! There's a button in my lunch!'
'Well, you did ask for a jacket potato . . . !'

A worker on a building site rushed up to the foreman. 'Gaffer! Gaffer!' he cried. 'Someone's just dropped a trowel from the top of the scaffolding and sliced my ear off!' Immediately the foreman organized a search party to find the ear in the hope that surgeons might be able to sew it on again. 'Here it is!' cried one of the searchers, waving an ear. 'No, that's not it,' said the injured workman. 'Mine had a pencil behind it!'

The following letter was received by the managing director of Jerry Builders Ltd from one of his workmen:

Dear Sir,
Upon examining the storm damage to the roof of the Manor House, Nob Hill, I discovered that quite a number of tiles had blown off. Accordingly I fixed up a beam and pulley in order to hoist up three barrel-loads of tiles. Having repaired the roof I found that I had a lot of tiles left over. I therefore hoisted up the empty barrel, secured the line at ground level, climbed back up to the roof and filled the barrel with tiles. I then went down again and untied the line. Unfortunately the barrel, now being heavier than me, pulled me off my feet. Half-way up I met the barrel coming down and received a severe blow on the shoulder. The barrel continued downwards and I continued upwards where I banged my head sharply on the beam and got my hand jammed in the pulley. When the barrel hit the ground it burst open, spilling the tiles. This meant that I was now heavier than the barrel and so I began to fall. Half-way down I met the barrel coming up, sustaining a severe blow to the shins. Upon hitting the ground I landed on the tiles, which occasioned

me numerous deep cuts. Stunned by the pain I let go the line
and the barrel then fell giving me a heavy blow on the head
and landing me in hospital.

I respectfully request sick leave,

Yours faithfully,

Rufus Fallen

This'll Kill You!

or Dying of Laughter

Why did the baby monster push his father's finger into the light socket?
  'Cos he wanted Fizzy Pop.

What is the best way for a ghost-hunter to keep fit?
  He must exorcise regularly.

What do you call twin ghosts who keep ringing doorbells?
  Dead ringers.

What is the ghost's favourite kind of tune?
  A haunting melody.

Who put their point of view at the ghosts' press conference?
  A spooksman.

Who said 'Shiver me timbers!' on the ghost ship?
  The skeleton crew.

Why are a monster's fingers never more than eleven inches long?
  'Cos if they were twelve inches they'd be a foot.

Why is a turkey like an evil little creature?
  'Cos it's always a-gobblin' . . .

Where did Dracula keep his money?
  In a blood bank.

How does a witch tell the time?
  With a witch watch.

Why was Frankenstein never lonely?
  He was good at making friends.

Why did the skeleton go to the party?
  For a rattling good time!

Why are ghosts bad at telling lies?
　'Cos you can always see through them.

Why are vampires mad?
　'Cos they're bats.

What did the policeman say when he met the three-headed monster?
　' 'Ello, 'Ello, 'Ello!'

What is a gargoyle?
　Something you take for a sore throat.

Where do you find giant snails?
　On the end of giants' fingers.

What is the monsters' favourite football team?
　Slitherpool.

Why wouldn't the skeleton jump off the cliff?
　'Cos it had no guts.

What is Dracula's favourite pudding?
　Leeches and scream.

What is Dracula's favourite breakfast?
　Readyneck.

The Ghost teacher was showing the Kiddie Ghosts how to walk through walls. 'Now did you all follow that, Ghosties?' she asked. 'If not, I'll just go through it again...'

Why does Dracula live in a coffin?
　'Cos the rent is low.

What did one ghost say to the other ghost?
　'Do you believe in people?'

What does a monster eat after a tooth extraction?
　The dentist.

What trees do monsters like best?
　Cemetrees.

If you were surrounded by Dracula, Frankenstein's monster, a ghost and a werewolf, what would you be hoping?
　That you were at a fancy-dress party.

Why are monsters forgetful?
'Cos everything you tell them goes in one ear and out the others.

What is the best way to speak to a monster?
From a long distance.

Where do monsters study?
At ghoullege.

What do you call a friendly and handsome monster?
A failure.

What has webbed feet and fangs?
Count Quackula.

Why did Frankenstein's monster give up boxing?
'Cos he didn't want to spoil his looks.

Why is Baron Frankenstein good fun at parties?
'Cos he'll have you in stitches.

What do vampires cross the sea in?
Blood vessels.

What is the best thing to do if a monster breaks down your front door?
Run out through the back door.

What do monsters put on their roast beef?
Grave-y.

What is a ghost's favourite drink?
Demonade.

What kind of ices do monsters prefer?
I-screams for help.

Did you hear about the stupid ghost?
He climbed over walls.

Where do monsters travel?
From ghost to ghost.

Why is Dracula so unpopular?
'Cos he's a pain in the neck.

What did the vampire say to the dentist after he'd had all his teeth out?
'Fangs for the memory!'

Can a toothless vampire still bite you?
   No, but he can give you a nasty suck!

Why did the landlord of a wine bar refuse to serve gin to a ghost?
   'Cos he didn't have a licence to serve spirits.

What do ghosts like to play at parties?
   Haunt and seek.

'Don't eat with your fingers, dear' said the Mummy ghost to the little ghost. 'Use the shovel!'

Why did the baby monster push his father in the freezer?
   'Cos he wanted frozen pop.

Travellers' Tales

Pilot: 'Mayday! Mayday! Starboard engine on fire!'
Ground Control: 'State your height and position.'
Pilot: 'I'm five feet eight and I'm sitting in the cockpit.'

'Last time my wife and I travelled on the ferry from Newhaven to Dieppe we had six meals.'
   'Six meals for that short crossing?'
   'Three down and three up.'

The young midshipman was being examined on his seamanship. 'Now, then, Scuttle,' said the examiner, 'you are about to enter harbour when a severe storm blows up. What do you do?'
   'I don't try to enter harbour, Sir. I let go an anchor and ride out the storm.'
   'Very good. But supposing the storm abates, you try and haul up the anchor and the chain snaps — and another storm blows up. What do you do?'
   'I'd throw out the spare anchor, Sir.'
   'Excellent. Now, the second storm abates; you try and raise the spare anchor, and again the chain snaps just as a third storm blows up. What do you do?'
   'I'd throw out a third anchor, Sir.'
   'Just a minute. Where are you getting all these anchors from?'
   'The same place you're getting the storms.'

'When we got to Benidorm the hotel was so full I had to sleep on a door across two trestles.'
   'Was it comfortable?'
   'Oh, yes. But a bit draughty round the letter-box.'

A motorist who had the misfortune to run over a woman's dog was extremely apologetic. 'I really am most terribly sorry, madam,' he said. 'I will of course replace your dog.'
   'If you like,' she replied, 'but are you any good at catching rats?'

An extremely rich businessman found himself in a small Lancashire hotel where his wealth and importance seemed to be quite unknown, and to his chagrin he was treated with no more and no less respect than any other guest. Determined to show his worth, at breakfast he said loudly to the waiter, 'Bring me £10 worth of bacon and eggs!' Not a whit abashed, the waiter said, 'Sorry, sir, but we don't serve half-portions!'

A French hitch-hiker in England was delighted when a motorist stopped at his thumbing signal. 'Want a lift, do you?' asked the motorist.

'Oui, oui,' agreed the Frenchman.

'Not in my car you don't!'

An American visitor to England was wandering round a small county town, and got into conversation with a local. 'What do you do for entertainment round here?' he asked. 'Is there a cinema?'

'No, no cinema,' said the local.

'A theatre?'

'No, no theatre.'

'A disco?'

'No, no disco.'

'So what is there in this town?'

'Well, we lads like to go to the grocers' shop and watch the bacon slicer.'

'That's fun, is it?'

'Well, she's a lovely girl.'

Another American visitor was being taken round Blackpool in a taxi. 'What's that building?' he asked. 'That's t'Town Hall, sir.' said the taxi-driver. 'The Town Hall?' said the American scornfully. 'Why we've got chip shops as big as that in the States!' They drove on for a while, and the American visitor said, 'And what's that building?' 'That's the Museum, sir,' said the taxi-driver. 'The Museum?' sneered the American. 'Why we've got chip shops as big as that back in the States.' So they drove on for a while longer until they came to the Blackpool Tower. 'So what the heck's that?' asked the American, to which the taxi-driver replied, 'That's a vinegar bottle for one of your chip shops!'

A motorist driving through the country stopped for a hitch-hiker who was holding the halter of a cow. 'I can give you a lift,' he said, 'but I can't take your cow.'

'Don't worry,' said the hitch-hiker, 'she'll follow us in her own time.'

So the hitch-hiker got in and the motorist started up. He drove at thirty miles an hour and the cow lolloped along behind him; he drove at forty miles an hour and the cow was still lolloping along behind him; he drove at fifty miles an hour yet the cow was somehow managing to keep pace with him. But he noticed in his mirror that the cow seemed to be tiring as her tongue was hanging out of her mouth. 'I'm worried about your cow,' said the motorist to his passenger, 'her tongue is hanging out of her mouth to the right.'

'Oh, that's all right,' said the hitch-hiker, 'that means she's going to overtake . . . !'

A man in the United States decided to make some money by getting himself run over. He stood at a bus stop and stuck his leg out so that when the bus arrived it ran him over. He was in hospital for three months and received $50,000 in compensation. Then he went to France and tried the same trick, this time receiving 200,000 francs in compensation. But when he came to Britain and stood at a bus stop with his leg sticking out he died of pneumonia . . .

A man and his friend were driving through the centre of town, and the driver's handling of the car was decidedly erratic. 'Tell me, Joey,' said his increasingly perturbed friend, 'why do you shut your eyes every time we come to a red light?'

'Why not?' retorted Joey. 'When you've seen one you've seen 'em all . . . !'

A traveller stranded in the desert asked a passerby for water. 'Sorry,' said the passerby, 'I have no water. Only ties which I am taking to market.' The traveller staggered on through the burning sands and met another passerby. 'Water' he gasped, 'Please, give me water!'

'I have no water,' said the second passerby. 'Only these ties which I am taking to market.' Nearly dead from thirst the traveller met a third passerby — but he was also only taking ties to market. And so the wretched traveller lurched on, half-dead from thirst, until to his joy he saw an hotel! He crawled into the lobby on his hands and knees and croaked out, 'Water! For the love of Allah, give me water!'

'Sorry, sir,' said the hall porter. 'We don't allow anyone in without a tie!'

Having asked for shelter for the night at a monastery the traveller was surprised and delighted at being given a magnificent supper of succulent fish and chips. 'That was absolutely superb!' he enthused to the monk who had been serving him. 'That piece of fish was wonderful, and beautifully cooked. And as for the chips — they were the tastiest chips I've ever had in my life. Well done, Brother.' 'Oh, you must thank Brother Ambrose for those,' came the reply. 'I'm the fish friar — he's the chip monk . . .'

A man sat on a train chewing gum and staring vacantly into space, when suddenly an old lady sitting opposite said, 'It's no good you talking to me, young man. I'm stone deaf!'

Fifty Irishmen were travelling on a train. 'Sure and it's too crowded in this compartment,' said the leader. 'The next one's empty — Let's use that one.' So at the next stop the fifty Irishmen alighted — and all promptly went into the empty compartment!

'You deliberately drove into my car!' said the first motorist to the second. 'Why did you do it?'

'I saw that sticker in your back window,' came the reply. 'It says "Give Blood" so I thought I'd give you some of mine!'

As the bus arrived at the stop, a man in the front of the queue took out his eye, bounced it hard on the pavement, caught it, put it back in his eye and boarded the bus.

'What did you do that for?' asked the amazed conductor.

'I just wanted to see,' replied the man, 'if there was any room on top!'

'I got a puncture in the rear tyre of my bike yesterday.'
  'Hard luck. Did you mend it?'
  'No, I just raised the seat.'

Just as the Jumbo jet was about to take off, a nervous old lady called for an air-hostess. 'I've never been in an aeroplane before,' she said. 'Tell me, my dear, what happens if we run out of fuel?'
  'Don't worry, madam,' replied the cheeky young woman. 'We all get out and push!'

Mr Simple was told at the Jobcentre that there was a vacancy for a bus-driver. 'But I can't drive,' he said. 'Never mind,' replied the clerk, 'they will train you.' So off went Mr Simple to the bus depot; he was accepted for training and in a few weeks had passed his driving test. As he was taking his bus out on his first shift he said to the Inspector, 'Where's the conductor?' 'Oh, we don't have conductors any longer,' said the Inspector. 'You have to collect the fares yourself.'
  So off went Mr Simple, driving confidently but carefully. But half an hour later the Inspector was appalled to receive a phone call from the manager of the local Woolworth store. 'Get over here!' screamed the manager. 'One of your buses has driven smack through the front of my shop!'
  The Inspector hurtled along to the scene of the accident, and sure enough, there was Mr Simple's bus embedded in the front of Woolworth's! No-one had been hurt, but there was broken glass and debris all over the pavement and the bus was almost completely wrecked. 'What on earth happened?' yelled the Inspector to the wretched Mr Simple. 'I don't know, guv,' he answered. 'When the bus crashed I was upstairs collecting fares!'

Whenever there is a road accident each driver involved has to write a report of the occurrence for the insurance company. The following are actual quotations from some of these reports:

  'Coming home, I drove into the wrong house and collided with a tree I didn't have.'

  'I thought my window was down, but I found it was up when I put my hand through it.'

  'I collided with a stationary lorry coming the other way.'

  'A van backed through my windscreen into my wife's face.'

  'A pedestrian hit me and went under my car.'

  'He was all over the road, and I had to swerve a number of times before I hit him.'

  'In an attempt to kill a fly I drove into a telephone pole.'

  'I had been driving my car for forty years when I fell asleep at the wheel.'

  'My car was legally parked as it backed into the other vehicle.'

  'An invisible car came out of nowhere, struck my vehicle and vanished.'

'I told the police that I was not injured, but on removing my hat I found that I had a fractured skull.'

'The pedestrian had no idea which direction to go, so I ran over him.'

'I saw the slow-moving, sad-faced old gentleman as he bounced off the bonnet of my car.'

'The indirect cause of this accident was the little chap in a small car with a moustache.'

'I was thrown from my car as it left the road. I was later found in a ditch by some cows.'

'The telephone pole was approaching fast and I was attempting to swerve out of its path when it struck my front.'

'I was on my way to the doctor when my rear end gave way, causing me to have an accident.'

'I pulled away from the side of the road, glanced at my mother-in-law and drove into the river.'

An intrepid explorer in the days of the old Wild West was captured by a Red Indian tribe notorious for their habit of skinning their victims alive. 'Before you die,' said the Big Chief solemnly, 'you are allowed one wish. What will it be, white man?'

'A fork, if you please,' said the explorer. Bemused, the Big Chief ordered a fork to be given to the white man, who immediately began plunging it into himself all over, saying, 'I'll make sure you don't make a canoe out of me!'